IMAGES
of America

ROCHE HARBOR

The homes of John S. and Louella McMillin and their son, Paul, hug the waterfront in this photograph found in a 1927 appraisal. Paul's home was later moved to a hill behind his parents' home, where it is now known as the McMillin Suites and affords a sweeping view of the gardens, harbor, and outer islands.

On the Cover: Roche Harbor takes on a festive flair as the USS *William Jones* (DD-380) is anchored in the harbor for a port visit and a passenger steamer ties up at the wharf. The hotel is in the foreground at right, looking out over the harbor, Pearl Pass, and Henry Island. The store and warehouse, built in 1923, help date this photograph. The *Jones* was built in 1919 by Bethlehem Steel, Roche Harbor's largest client.

IMAGES
of America

ROCHE HARBOR

Richard Walker

ARCADIA
PUBLISHING

Published by Arcadia Publishing
Charleston SC, Chicago IL, Portsmouth NH, San Francisco CA

Printed in the United States of America

Library of Congress Control Number: 2009920378

For all general information contact Arcadia Publishing at:
Telephone 843-853-2070
Fax 843-853-0044
E-mail sales@arcadiapublishing.com
For customer service and orders:
Toll-Free 1-888-313-2665

Visit us on the Internet at www.arcadiapublishing.com

For my Molly

CONTENTS

ACKNOWLEDGMENTS

Behind every successful author is an army of people, without whom a book would not be possible.

My wife Molly's love and encouragement buoyed me during the many hours required for this book. Many thanks to Rich Komen, co-owner of Roche Harbor, for his sponsorship of this project and for opening Roche Harbor's extensive archives to me. Brent Snow and Pat Carver of the Roche Harbor staff provided valuable research assistance. My editor, Sarah Higginbotham, was always accessible and helpful.

Mary McMillin Cooper, granddaughter of John S. and Louella Hiett McMillin, allowed me to study family letters and photographs that provided insight into McMillin family life. Wolf Bauer, Roche Harbor's chief engineer from 1936 to 1939, spent time with me to ensure I understood the lime production process and toured the old quarries with me. Advice provided by my friend and fellow journalist Mike Vouri proved spot on. Al Sundstrom, historian extraordinaire, knew where to find elusive photographs.

Numerous families opened their homes and lives to me, and to them I offer my lifelong gratitude: Sam Buck Sr., Julie Capron, Victor J. Capron III, Chester Cayou, Charles Chevalier, Anne Guthrie, Susan Anderson Harris, Lutie Hillaire, Teresa Tarte Tangney Kennedy, Joyce Tuck-Lowe, Bill and Bernice Mason, Dick and Barbara Nagaoka, Wilma Rimer, Cho and Sharonne Shimizu, and Neil Tarte.

I also appreciate the assistance of Steve Buck, Gwen Cole, Marie DiCristina, David Gibbs, Rick Guard, Janine Wells, and the San Juan Island Historical Museum's Mary Jean Cahail and Kevin Loftus.

Photographs not credited are provided courtesy of Roche Harbor and its archives.

INTRODUCTION

Roche Harbor has a rich history that influences it today.

It is a place of origin; archeological evidence shows humans have lived here at least 6,000 years.

It is a symbol of international peace, where a 12-year military occupation was ended in 1872 without a shot being fired in hostility.

It is a place with rich natural resources that in 1886 attracted a young visionary who built the largest lime manufacturing plant west of the Mississippi. Lime quarried here helped build cities along the West Coast and helped rebuild San Francisco after that city's devastating earthquake in 1906.

It is an environment that has long sustained human life, marine life, and wildlife.

San Juan Island is believed by the Lummi and Songhees people to be their place of origin. They and other Coast Salish peoples regularly harvested the island's rich resources from land and sea. Their village names and sites are well documented.

In 1845, the Hudson's Bay Company (HBC) was drawn to the island's expansive prairies and protected harbors and established a claim here; a salmon-curing station and a sheep ranch followed. The claim was also intended to bolster the British presence in the region. The British built the island's first roads—many of which are in use today—using Cowichan and Songhees First Nation laborers.

The international boundary agreed to in the Oregon Treaty of 1846 was unclear, and the presence of American and British settlers on the island led to tensions that were heightened when an American settler shot a Hudson's Bay Company boar rooting in his garden near what is now American Camp. Threats of arrest led to the presence of U.S. troops to protect the interests of American settlers; the British sent troops to protect their claim on the island. This led to a joint occupation (1859–1872) until the dispute could be resolved.

A German arbitration panel ruled 2-1 that the San Juan Islands belonged to the United States, and the British flag was lowered at English Camp, the last place in the continental United States where the British flag flew.

Lawyer John S. McMillin and his partners in the Tacoma Lime Company bought Roche Harbor from Richard and Robert Scurr in 1886; the brothers had established a lime quarry and kilns there, an expansion of the operation begun by British Royal Marines. It turned out that Roche Harbor sat on the largest and purest deposit of lime in the Northwest.

On December 8, 1886, Tacoma and Roche Harbor Lime Company was incorporated; it would later be known as Roche Harbor Lime and Cement Company. McMillin built the 20-room Hotel de Haro, reportedly an expansion of the Scurr brothers' bunkhouse, for his employees and guests. By 1889, a company town emerged—a lime factory, barns, barrel works, a church, a company store, docks, homes, offices, piers, a school, ships, and a warehouse. Workers were paid in scrip good at the company store, but they could draw their wages in currency when desired. Roche Harbor ultimately comprised the town (with autonomous electrical power and water systems), 12 miles of shoreline, and 4,000 forested acres that helped provide wood for the kilns.

As Roche Harbor became a powerful economic force on the islands, McMillin became politically and socially influential. He entertained elegantly and lavishly. He ran for the U.S. Senate in 1895. In 1904, he helped Port Townsend mayor Charles E. Coon in the latter's successful campaign for lieutenant governor; on April 23, 1904, the *Port Townsend Leader* referred to McMillin as San Juan County's "leading man." He served as a member of the state railroad commission—forerunner of the state utilities commission—from 1906 to 1908 and was a Republican National Convention delegate in 1924 and 1932.

By the 1930s, the lime industry waned because of the building slump caused by the Great Depression. McMillin died in 1936 and was succeeded by his son, Paul, who led the company during a period of changing markets and labor unrest.

In 1956, ownership of Roche Harbor passed to another visionary: Reuben J. Tarte, who with his family transformed the lime company town into a premier Northwest boating resort. They restored the old buildings, built the marina, and added recreational amenities. They started new traditions that continue today. Every sunset during summer, Roche Harbor hosts a colors ceremony that includes the lowering of the national flags and the playing of the national songs of Canada, Great Britain, and the United States.

In 1988, the Tartes sold Roche Harbor to grocer Verne Howard and restaurateur Rich Komen. Howard later sold out so he could concentrate on his other business interests. Komen now owns Roche Harbor in partnership with Saltchuk Resources, a Seattle maritime holding company.

In 2001, Komen's vision began to take shape: that of a village with permanent, year-round residents. New commercial buildings and residential neighborhoods have been developed, all in the architectural style of the early 1900s. The Roche Harbor Amphitheater is a venue for live entertainment. Westcott Bay Sculpture Park is located at the entrance to the village, on what was once McMillin's Bellevue Farm. The 19-acre sculpture park overlooks forest, meadow, rocky outcroppings, and wetlands and features a rotating exhibit of more than 100 sculptures.

The First Peoples of Roche Harbor still maintain ties to this place. In 2004 and 2008, Coast Salish canoes returned to Roche Harbor's beaches as part of the Canoe Journey, a gathering that keeps alive traditional travel upon the ancestral waters.

Well-preserved buildings at English Camp and a British cemetery on Mount Young are reminders of the military occupation. Roche Harbor's cemetery and mausoleum are silent reminders of the people who contributed to local life. Residents and visitors can hike Roche Harbor's old lime quarries and visit heritage buildings that bring that history to life.

History comes full circle at Roche Harbor. The events and the people of the past are as influential today as they were then. This is their story.

One day in 1938, Mary McMillin led tugboat builder Henry Foss and his associates on a tour of the Roche Harbor lime works and village. Shortly after, the *Calcite* arrived with a gift for Mary from Foss: this cedar canoe for her 16th birthday. She always treasured the show of appreciation, and her granddaughter uses the canoe today. Posey Island is in the background. (Mary McMillin Cooper collection.)

One

THIS PLACE CALLED WHELAALK

What we call Roche Harbor was already a thriving place when the British staked a claim on the island in 1845.

Roche Harbor was known by the Lummi and Songhees as Whelaalk and was believed to have been the original home of their first ancestor, Sweh-tuhn.

Relatives canoeing northeast from Sngeck-kuh on Cadboro Bay, across today's Haro Strait, would pass the village of Lhuh-lhee-ng'kwulh on Henry Island at the head of Open Bay.

Approaching Lhuh-lhee-ng'kwulh, canoe pullers might look east and see P'kweekh-eel-wuhlh on the point near the entrance to Mitchell Bay. Informants told anthropologist Wayne Suttles (1918–2005) that there were "big houses" and "a lot of Indians there" in the mid- and late 1800s.

Inside the pass between Lhuh-lhee-ng'kwulh and P'kweekh-eel-wuhlh is Garrison Bay, where the British established their camp. The Lummi and Songhees knew this place as Smuh-yuh. British Royal Marines dismantled a traditional cedar-plank house on what became the parade ground of their garrison, Dr. Julie Stein wrote in her book, *Exploring Coast Salish Prehistory*.

When John S. McMillin was quarrying lime at Roche Harbor, Tom Siuqwle'maltxw (pronounced she-kla-malt) and other Lummi people were living at an old village site 1 1/2 miles northeast on Speiden Channel. Informants told Suttles that the village had "10 large houses" in the mid- and late 1800s. Siuqwle'maltxw lived there until his death in 1900.

Directly north of Whelaalk was Kwuh-nuhs, a Saanich village on the east shore of Stuart Island's Reid Harbor occupied year-round as late as the 1880s.

The settlement era changed the island in many ways, but the First People continued to be a part of Whelaalk. They fished, helped build the island's roads and sheep runs, worked in the quarries, and attained positions of leadership in the community.

Today the descendants of Whelaalk's first residents return regularly to maintain cultural resources. They fish in their ancestral waters. Periodically, as part of the Canoe Journey, they come to Whelaalk's shores in traditional canoes, sing songs their ancestors knew, and speak the languages their ancestors spoke.

Reef-net fishing originated in the San Juan Islands and is practiced today by descendants of Whelaalk's First People. A net was suspended between canoes in the path of the salmon. Artificial reefs made from cedar bark, nettle fibers, and beach grass guided the migrating salmon into the net. When the salmon swam in, the scoop-shaped net was raised, and the fish were trapped. (Wilma Rimer collection.)

Songhees leader Michael Cooper and his family are pictured here around 1900 in Victoria, British Columbia. The Songhees had about 10 villages on the west side of San Juan Island when settlers began arriving in the 1850s. Cooper (1864–1936) was born on San Juan to a Songhees mother and a Royal Marine father. Cooper led the Songhees Nation from 1893 to 1935 and helped establish a Songhees reserve in Victoria in 1911. (Buswell collection, Center for Pacific Northwest Studies.)

Patrick George, wearing a ceremonial robe, speaks at a potlatch on the Lummi reservation in this *c.* 1940 photograph. George, whose Lummi name was Slalhilton, was born at Whelaalk about 1876. His descendants visit the islands regularly to care for and protect cultural resources. His granddaughter, Lutie Hillaire, said her grandmother told her, "We were here yesterday, we're here today, we're going to be here tomorrow." (Buswell collection, Center for Pacific Northwest Studies.)

Patrick George's wife, Agnes, and others are photographed on the Lummi reservation in 1942 displaying regalia that would have been familiar to the First Peoples of Whelaalk. From left to right are (first row) Julius Charles (wearing hair hat and paddle shirt), Annie Pierre, Nellie Charles, and Mrs. John Jones; (second row) Chief August Martin, Felix Solomon, and Agnes George (wearing headdress with glass beadwork). (Buswell collection, Center for Pacific Northwest Studies.)

The Chevalier family, pictured on Speiden Island in 1911, is, from left to right, (seated) Caroline Chevalier, Edward Chevalier, and Mary Chevalier; (kneeling) Elmer Chevalier and Alfred Chevalier; (standing) Henry Balam, William Chevalier, and Ellen Chevalier. Alfred's Indian name, pronounced pa-KWAL-us, means "wide eyes," a reference to his ability to spot fish while reef-netting. He received the name from his uncle, Isaac Jack. (Wilma Rimer collection.)

Children from the Chevalier and Mordhorst families row from Speiden Island to Stuart Island for school in 1902. The passengers are believed to be General Cayou; Alfred, Ellen, and William Chevalier; and Adeline and Ollie Mordhorst. The men grew up to fish at reef-net sites that their families fished for centuries and also worked for Roche Harbor in their young adulthood. (Wilma Rimer collection.)

This is an early-1900s photograph of Roche Harbor at low tide, looking out toward the boathouse. The lime company's shipyard is visible in the background at right. This scene would have been familiar to workers rowing home to Speiden and Stuart Islands. The company tug, *Roche Harbor*, is moored at center. (Wilma Rimer collection.)

From left to right, General Cayou, Lewie Smith, and William Chevalier pose for a photograph prior to World War I. Cayou and Smith were Chevalier's uncles. Their families grew up on Stuart Island but moved around the San Juan Islands to farm, fish, and hunt. Family members traveled often by canoe to Vancouver Island, British Columbia, for family reunions and ceremonial gatherings. (Wilma Rimer collection.)

At right, Caroline "Toots" Chevalier (1908–2004) enjoys a school picnic in Roche Harbor. In an August 13, 2002, story in the *Seattle Post-Intelligencer*, she told how her mother taught her to catch and smoke fish and pick berries. On Stuart Island, "there was nothing but Indian camps," she said. "Saanich, from Canada, used to come up in big long canoes; you could hear them singing on the water." (Wilma Rimer collection.)

Toots Chevalier rowed daily to Roche Harbor with lunch for Norman Franklin Mills during their courtship. They married on October 23, 1937, in Friday Harbor. Mills was born in Roche Harbor in 1914 and, like his father, worked for the lime company. After he and Toots married, Mills became a boat builder, a commercial fisherman, and a farmer. They spent much of their life together on Stuart Island. (Wilma Rimer collection.)

From left to right, Chester, Susie, and Roger Cayou were the children of Gen. Scott Cayou and Sara Jack. General Cayou cut wood with a crosscut saw for Roche Harbor. Chester bagged lime for Roche Harbor until he was drafted into the army during World War II, when he served with distinction in France. He later moved to the Swinomish reservation and became a longtime member of the Swinomish Senate. (Wilma Rimer collection.)

Susie Cayou takes the family dog for a boat ride off Stuart Island. Her family was firmly planted in two worlds: relatives spoke the Saanich language and a grandmother was married to the head fisherman of the Mitchell Bay Indians. Her uncle, Henry Cayou (1869–1959), served on the San Juan County Commission, owned a cannery on Orcas Island's West Sound, and was perhaps the most successful fisherman in the state. (Wilma Rimer collection.)

Mary Smith Chevalier (1878–1966) rakes clams on Waldron Island in 1947. Her father, Robert Smith, was a Royal Marine during the joint military occupation; after the boundary dispute ended, he settled on Speiden Island, across Speiden Passage from Roche Harbor. Her Native mother, Lucy Jack, spoke Saanich and had long ties to the islands. (Rick Guard collection.)

Marjorie Chevalier Workman (1922–2004), granddaughter of Mary Chevalier, cleans a buck she hunted. She had vivid memories of Coast Salish canoes slicing through Haro Strait between Canada's Gulf Islands and America's San Juans, of building salmon traps and sewing fishing nets out of cedar bark, and of harvesting seaweed for market. "Everything was so plentiful around here— herring, clams, salmon," she said. "That was our way of life." (Rick Guard collection.)

Two

THE SETTLEMENT ERA

The London Times, in a story reprinted in the October 18, 1859, *New York Times*, wrote that Americans in the Pacific Northwest were subjecting British Columbia to a "reign of rowdyism" and nibbling "at the possessions of her Britannic Majesty."

"The notion of disputing our right to an island which has been in the possession of the Hudson's Bay Co. for an indefinite time . . . and of doing this simply because it was pretended that an American had been arrested for an outrage on the Company's property, is something new in the annals of military achievements."

The "outrage" was committed in June 1859 by Lyman Cutlar, who established a claim on the HBC's Belle Vue Farm on southwest San Juan Island. Cutlar shot an HBC-owned boar that had been rooting in his garden. Belle Vue Farm manager Charles J. Griffin threatened Cutlar with arrest.

Tensions had been building for years. An 1846 treaty drew the international boundary down "the middle of the channel which separates the continent from Vancouver's Island," neglecting the archipelago in the middle of said channel.

On Great Britain's behalf, the HBC had posted a notice of possession near San Juan Island's Cattle Pass in 1845 and established a salmon-curing station and a sheep ranch there.

On March 2, 1853, Washington Territory was broken off from Oregon Territory and, later that year, Island County (including the San Juan Islands) was formed. The San Juans became part of Whatcom in 1854. By 1859, there were about 25 Americans on San Juan Island, settled on land claims they expected the United States to recognize as valid. The British saw them as squatters.

After Cutlar was threatened with arrest, U.S. brigadier general William S. Harney ordered Company D, 9th Infantry, to the island to prevent British officials from imposing jurisdiction over U.S. citizens. Gov. James Douglas of British Columbia dispatched a law enforcement officer to order the troops off the island.

The heightening situation appalled military leaders from both countries, and a joint occupation was proposed until ownership could be determined. On March 21, 1860, a Royal Marine Light Infantry contingent landed at the place the Lummi and Songhees knew as Smuh-yuh.

The First People of Smuh-yuh left behind evidence of their occupation dating back at least 2,000 years and up to the time of the Royal Marines' arrival. Here marines plant a vegetable garden near the former site of a longhouse. In his diary, marine sergeant William Joy described a shell midden 10 feet high, 35 to 40 feet wide, and 120 yards long. (San Juan Island National Historical Park [SJINHP].)

James Prevost, commander of the HMS *Satellite*, recommended Smuh-yuh as the site of the British military camp based on a visit during the Boundary Commission's survey of the island. The site was in a sheltered bay, offered rich natural resources, and was convenient—only 20 nautical miles from Fort Victoria. The HMS *Boxer*, pictured, delivered provisions to the camp once a month. (SJINHP.)

This navigational chart was created by the Royal Navy during the boundary survey in 1857 and was updated as a chart of "Roche Harbour and its Approaches" in 1863. The Royal Navy expanded the boundaries of its military reservation to include Roche Harbor after its lime works was established there. In response, the U.S. Army expanded its military reservation to include nearly the entire Cattle Point peninsula. (SJINHP.)

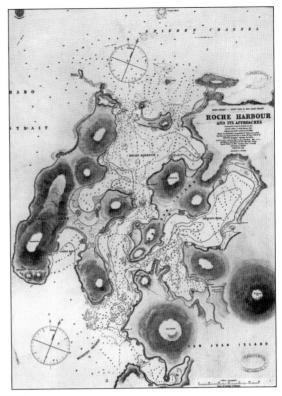

Royal Navy lieutenant Richard Roche (1831–1888) is credited with establishing the first lime works at Whelaalk, which the British renamed in his honor. "A splendid article of lime, white as chalk, is now being made at San Juan Island," the *Pioneer and Democrat* newspaper in Olympia reported on September 28, 1860. "The stone from which it is manufactured is almost inexhaustible." (Royal British Columbia Museum.)

In this pre-1867 photograph of the Royal Marine camp, the site has been cleared and buildings erected, but visitors would recognize Sgt. William Joy's earlier description of the site: "The brush wood grew quite down to the water's edge, in the rear the forest was growing in undisturbed tranquility, yellow Pine, White Pine, cedar, Alder and Willows." (SJINHP.)

Coast Salish–style canoes rest on the beach near the steamer dock around 1868. National Park historian Michael Vouri said there is no record of trade visits at the site, although visual artifacts depict Coast Salish canoes in these waters during the British occupation. From left to right are the commissary, an unidentified building, a blockhouse, barracks, and laundress' quarters. The grove of cedars and junipers at center exists today. (SJINHP.)

Capt. William Addis Delacombe, commandant of the Royal Marine detachment at San Juan, relaxes with his family on the steps of their home on Officers Hill. The home had nine rooms, a kitchen, a room for the family nurse, two verandas, and a view of Haro Strait. The lawn provided a venue for badminton, croquet, and tennis. The house was destroyed by fire in 1894.

At the camp, marines and guests enjoyed the abundant resources that had long sustained Smuh-yuh's original residents. Anglican Bishop George Hills wrote in his journal on February 2, 1861: "The Dinner at the Mess today proved the value of the island." The menu included venison, "which is always to be had for a walk in the early morning," as well as candlefish, duck, and salmon. (SJINHP.)

On October 21, 1872, an arbitration panel led by Emperor Wilhelm I of Germany voted 2-1 to award possession of the San Juan Islands to the United States. On November 21, the Royal Marines lowered their nation's flag and left the island. But the permanent, non-Native settlement of Smuh-yuh was set. This photograph was taken in 1872. (SJINHP.)

English-born Isaac Sandwith (1852–1923) moved to San Juan Island with his parents in 1867, married Sarah Porter of Victoria in 1873, and by 1890 had a home on Mount Young, a 200-acre ranch, and a 640-acre sheep range. He later served as a county commissioner. From left to right are (first row) Hannah, Sarah, Mary Jane, and Joseph Sandwith; (second row) Sarah and Isaac Sandwith, Jim Fleming, and Joe Fleming. (Molly Sandwith Liebman collection.)

Three years after British troops left, William Crook, a 40-year-old English-born farmer, homesteaded the former military camp. With him were his wife, Mary; daughter, Mary, born in 1871 in Nebraska; and son, James, born in 1873 in Wyoming. Another daughter, Rhoda, was born in 1880 at this farm. The family lived in several military buildings at the camp until they built this house in 1903. (SJINHP.)

The Crook family's farm altered the former military and indigenous landscape. The family preserved the blockhouse and other buildings, but the Royal Marines' garden, built near the site of a longhouse, is gone, replaced by an orchard. The former military camp was purchased by the U.S. National Park Service in 1966 and the garden replanted in 1972.

Richard and Robert Scurr bought Roche Harbor from merchant Israel Katz in 1879 and continued the lime works the British had started. After they sold the lime works to McMillin and the Tacoma Lime Company in 1886, they worked for competitor Henry Cowell and built this home on nearby White Point. When Richard died on February 1, 1909, McMillin's boat, *Calcite*, transported his body to Friday Harbor for interment. (San Juan Historical Museum.)

A year after his brother died, Robert Scurr (1833–1913) married a young teacher, Nettie Hill (1868–1935), and they lived at White Point. Although he died three years after they married, Mrs. Scurr, 45 at the time, never married again. Here the family gathers at the Scurr home. From left to right are Nettie Scurr; Nettie's brother and sister-in-law, Ensign and Elizabeth Hill; Robert Scurr; Mrs. Scurr's father, Edgar Hill; and Ella Stevenson, Mrs. Scurr's aunt. (Susan Anderson collection.)

Three

LIME

SAN JUAN ISLAND'S GOLD

To understand how precise a visionary John S. McMillin was, pretend that it's 1886, look at the hills above the village, and imagine what he saw on his first visit: limestone deposits 350 feet above sea level, land for kilns below; room for barreling and warehousing, and a deep-water harbor.

With capital, the Scurr brothers' operation could be expanded into a highly efficient gravity-based system: Rock would be blasted in the quarries, broken by hand into 8- to 12-inch pieces, and loaded into railcars that would roll to a trestle above the kilns. The rocks would be dropped into the kilns to be burned for four hours at 2,000 degrees, releasing carbon dioxide from the rock. The resulting quicklime would drop down into a compartment to cool. At the right time, a lever would be pulled, and the quicklime would drop down a chute into the barreling room and then be transported to the adjacent warehouse to await loading onto a ship.

Within a few years, McMillin's Tacoma and Roche Harbor Lime Company was the largest west of the Mississippi. Its efficiency was widely reported in the press.

British Royal Marines operated a lime works here from 1860 to 1872, when they left the island. According to title records, Joseph Ruff obtained a homestead patent on 155.35 acres at Roche Harbor on April 25, 1877. He sold to merchant Israel Katz on February 27, 1878, for $3,200. Perhaps because of his commitments to his stores in Port Townsend, Friday Harbor, Argyle, and San Juan Town, Katz sold his Roche Harbor holdings to Robert Scurr on June 6, 1879, for $2,189; Scurr was later joined by his brother, Richard.

The Scurrs expanded the operation begun by British Royal Marines. More partners joined the company: Donald and Alexander Ross in 1882 and Colin Ross in 1884. On January 28, 1886, McMillin bought Colin Ross's interest in Roche Harbor for $7,500. On August 18, he bought the Scurrs's and Donald and Alexander Ross's interests for $30,000—quite a return on their initial investment. But Roche Harbor would pay dividends to its new owners; it sat on the largest and purest deposit of lime in the Northwest.

McMillin knew the value of limestone. He was born on October 28, 1855, in Sugar Grove, Tippecanoe County, Indiana. His state's quarries produced limestone used, from 1827 through his young adulthood, to build Indiana University in Bloomington, many of Indiana's official buildings, most state capitol buildings in the United States, and bridges and tunnels for an expanding railroad system.

McMillin received an undergraduate degree from Indiana Asbury University (now DePauw) in 1876. He and his childhood sweetheart, Louella Hiett, married on June 5, 1877. The young couple experienced their first heartbreak when their son, John Hiett McMillin, died after birth on July 16, 1878. McMillin earned a master's degree from Indiana Asbury in 1879 and practiced law. Another son, Fred Hiett McMillin, was born on September 16, 1880.

In January 1884, the McMillins followed his brother and family—the Reverend William B. McMillin, his wife Arietta, and son Clifford—west to a region experiencing an economic boom in anticipation of statehood.

John S. McMillin (1855–1936) invested in the Tacoma Lime Company after moving to Tacoma in 1884. After investigating the limestone deposits at Roche Harbor, he and his partners bought the Scurr brothers' lime company for $37,500. McMillin sought California industrialist Henry Cowell's financial help to develop the operation. Cowell turned him down but started a rival operation on the island and later bought stock in McMillin's company.

Henry Cowell (c. 1819–1903) was a tough competitor. The Massachusetts-born industrialist made his fortune in the lime industry in California and expanded into Washington. After McMillin invested in an efficient barrel-making system, Cowell sued, alleging McMillin didn't keep him apprised as a shareholder. McMillin testified Cowell would have used the information to his rival company's benefit. The court ruled in McMillin's favor. (The Museum of Art and History at the McPherson Center, Santa Cruz, California.)

Workers use a double-hand crank to hoist and move rock from the area where kilns 7, 8, and 9 would be built in 1890. By 1891, Roche Harbor increased production from 150 to 750 barrels of lime a day and was worth $1 million, about $23 million in 2007 dollars. By comparison, Cowell's two kilns at San Juan produced 230 barrels per day. (Wallie Funk collection, Anacortes History Museum, Anacortes, Washington.)

In August 1889, the *West Shore* magazine wrote of Roche Harbor's employee cottages, "Good, roomy houses, hard finished and neatly painted, are rented at $7.50 per month to employees having families. . . . It would seem as though this were the workman's Utopia." Single workers roomed in nearby bunkhouses.

Roche Harbor. From Pearl pass. Quarry. Kilns. Warf and Hotel

This pre-1890 panorama shows the "systematic development of the property . . . at once begun" by Tacoma and Roche Harbor Lime Company, as reported in the *West Shore*. The dock was 450 feet long "with a front of sixty-six feet." Steel rails "were laid on a trestle leading from the quarry to the kilns." By this time, the company was valued at $1 million, the *West Shore* reported.

Roche Harbor is pictured about 1903. From left to right are homes, the Hotel de Haro, buildings for barreling and sacking lime, the warehouse, the company store facing the water, and the kilns. At that time, Seattle attorney and journalist Honor Wilhelm described the bustling company town as "a bright and inviting place. The pure white buildings with the dark green of the surrounding hills give it a beautiful setting."

This early photograph gives a close look at the efficiency of Roche Harbor's lime manufacturing operation. Train cars dropped quarried limestone into the kilns to be burned. When finished, the processed lime dropped down into coolers and then down a chute to be barreled. The barrels were loaded onto a cart pulled by horse on a track to the warehouse on the wharf to await shipment.

Roche Harbor's activity generated widespread interest. John McMillin, an avid photographer, took this picture of guests on tour on July 31, 1922. A comparison of this photograph to other images of the lime works shows constant evolution in an attempt to boost efficiency and productivity. Adding to the excitement, "At all times, ocean-going and local craft are to be seen at the docks," journalist Honor Wilhelm wrote.

A scow is loaded with barrels and spalls for transport to market or for loading onto a ship at anchor. Spalls are lime rocks too small to be burned in the kilns. Smelters used spalls as a flux in steelmaking; a flux removes impurities from steel and increases slag formation. Next to the warehouse at right is Roche Harbor's first store.

Here is an early view of the harbor from above the kilns. Beyond the kilns, Roche Harbor looked as much a seaside village as it did a company town, with a church, hotel, gardens, school, and store. Leo A. Borah wrote in the February 1933 *National Geographic*: "At Roche Harbor, a poet's dream of white houses amid green lawns and flowers about a crescent beach, it was surprising to find one of the largest lime plants in Washington."

In 1889, Roche Harbor began manufacturing barrels from staves, or narrow strips of wood placed edge to edge. Fire destroyed the plant on September 10, 1892, as it was undergoing conversion to staveless barrel manufacture. A new plant was built, and manufacture resumed in April 1893. From 1895 to 1898, the Staveless Barrel Company made $35,766.27 in profit, offsetting the lime company's losses during the national economic depression of that period.

At the Staveless Barrel Company, logs were cut into pieces the length of a barrel and revolved against a knife so "that a shaving the proper shape, thickness and bevel is pared off, ready to be made into a barrel." The company made barrels for lime as well as candy, coffee, fire clay, and oatmeal. In 1901, it had a capacity of 4,000 barrels a day and employed 50 people.

Coopers, or barrel makers, were vital to Roche Harbor, whose kilns could produce at least 1,300 barrels of lime per day, according to a company prospectus dated December 1915. "Barring all delays for repairs, etc., [the plant] can easily produce 400,000 barrels of lime per annum." Coopers stand amid barrels in various stages of completion. Unfortunately, fire again visited the barrel plant that year.

This 1930s aerial photograph shows roads leading from the quarries to the kilns, the warehouse, the hotel and gardens, the church and cottages, and the shipyard in the distance. As early as 1860, the press touted Roche Harbor's limestone deposit as being "inexhaustible." But by the mid-1930s, it became clear that the mining operation was running its course, according to Wolf Bauer, chief engineer from 1936 to 1939. (Mary McMillin Cooper collection.)

The elevation of the quarries above the kilns made moving the quarried limestone relatively easy. After powdermen blasted rock loose in the quarry, skilled quarrymen would break the larger rocks into 8- to 12-inch pieces that would be hand-loaded into empty railcars that had been pulled to the quarries by horses. Ultimately 11 quarries would be mined.

Railcars loaded with limestone were driven by gravity down to a steam locomotive, which pulled them along a trestle parallel to the top of the kilns. There the rocks would be dumped into the kilns for burning. This was the only locomotive on the San Juan Islands.

Company president John McMillin pays a visit to a glory hole in one of the quarries in 1931. In the 1920s, the glory hole became a common method of extracting limestone. In glory hole mining, a steep-sided, funnel-shaped surface excavation is connected to tunnels below it. Rocks blasted off the sides of the excavation fall into the tunnels and into railcars.

The introduction of heavy equipment initiated another form of limestone extraction: stripping. Stripping was done by a steam shovel mounted on Caterpillar tractors. The steam shovel removed the "overburden" of rock and soil that lay above the limestone to be mined. This material was loaded onto railcars or trucks and hauled away.

Rail was ultimately replaced by gasoline-powered trucks, but each change in technology benefited from Roche Harbor's natural setting. A company prospectus reported, "The works are built on an incline so that the product works downward by gravity from the time the stone is blasted out in the quarry above the kilns until the finished product is delivered in barrels in the hold of a vessel."

In this undated picture, likely from the 1920s, workers dump a load of rocks from their truck into a kiln.

Merle Boyce and his 1950 or 1951 International deliver about two cords of wood to Roche Harbor's wood yard. The yard maintained a supply of 1,000 cords of wood yielded from the island's 4,000 acres of forestland as well as from foresters on other islands. Merle Boyce, Al Sundstrom, and Del Tift cut wood using crosscut saws sharpened nightly by Tift. (Nola Nash collection.)

Wood, cut into rounds or splits measuring 1 foot by 4 feet, is stacked and ready to fire the adjacent kilns. Seven of eight kilns were operated 24 hours a day, seven days a week. Each kiln used three cords of wood a day, Wolf Bauer said. Each kiln was lined in brick and jacketed in iron with an insulation of ash and gravel between the brick and iron jacket.

Firemen load wood into the furnace, which sent a constant torrent of heat—2,000 degrees—into the kiln to burn carbon dioxide and water vapor from the limestone. The resulting quicklime weighed 40 percent less than the original stone. The fire had to be skillfully regulated; burned rock was useless. It was "hard and sweaty work, especially in the summer," according to Bauer. "Nightshift was often preferred."

In the drawing and barreling department, workers fill barrels with cooled quicklime that comes down the chute and then hammer the barrel lids into place. Filled barrels were then taken to the warehouse to be stored until shipped. This part of the operation is at the same level as the wharf and warehouses.

At left one can see how the coopers delivered barrels down to the drawing and barreling department to be filled. Quicklime was first used primarily as a building material in mortar and stucco, but in the 20th century, it became widely used in agricultural, chemical, and metallurgical industries, with more than a hundred applications.

In the background, wearing a suit, company president John McMillin watches as quicklime comes down a chute for barreling while, in the foreground, a worker affixes a barrel lid. Quicklime was used in cement and mortar, pulverized for use as a soil conditioner, crushed for aggregate and road beds, and used in the manufacture of glass, paint, paper, plastics, and tiles.

Each barrel contained 200 pounds of quicklime; bags contained 100 pounds of lime powder. Bauer said that when he joined the company, Roche Harbor had stopped barreling lime and was bagging only. At that time, the company was doing its own crushing and pulverizing, allowing for most quicklime to be shipped in bags.

Calvin Morrill (1921–1960) bags lime at a hopper; filled lime bags were taken by front-end loader to the warehouse for shipping. Morrill had strong ties to Roche Harbor: his father, P. C. Morrill, served as John McMillin's personal secretary from 1905 to 1911. His uncle, Victor J. Capron, became the company doctor in 1898 and continued to see patients here after he moved to Friday Harbor to found a hospital and serve as mayor.

Barrels and sacks of lime are stored in the warehouse, ready for shipping. "It is a grand sight to see long rows of barrels piled high in these warerooms, one of which is 30x200 in size, and the other at the wharf 36x140 feet in dimensions, having in all a capacity of stowing away over 20,000 barrels," the *San Juan Islander* newspaper reported in 1901.

The horse at right pulls a sled with about 21 barrels of lime from the warehouse to the dock to be shipped. Considering that each barrel weighed about 200 pounds, this load weighed about 4,200 pounds, but movement was eased by a track.

Barrels on the Roche Harbor wharf await loading onto ships; a tug is tied up alongside. The *San Juan Islander* newspaper reported in 1901 of the company's shipping operations: "the company operates a brigantine, the *Wm. G. Irwin*, of 550 tons burden, which makes a monthly trip to San Francisco; also a steam tug of 60 tons, the *Roche Harbor*, besides five barges."

BIRDSEYE VIEW OF DOCKS AND COMPANY'S FLEET OF VESSELS TUGS AND LAUNCHES.

A bird's-eye view of Roche Harbor's docks shows its fleet of boats, ships, and tugs. The ship at dock resembles the *Archer*, the ship at anchor, the *Wm. G. Irwin*. The *Archer* was replaced by the *Star of Chile* about 1915; the *Wm. G. Irwin* was sold and replaced by a freighter. The *Wm. G. Irwin* was burned for a movie off of Catalina Island in May 1926.

Lime is hoisted onto a ship as men ready a cargo boom for another load at the Roche Harbor wharf in 1925. A company prospectus described Roche Harbor's location as ideal for marine trade: "right upon the regular highway of vessels plying between Puget Sound, British Columbia and Alaskan ports, also to and from California, Hawaiian Islands and all other ports on the Pacific Ocean."

Lime is lightered, or transferred by barge, to the *Silverado*. Lightering was required if a ship had a deep draft or if the tide was low. Lightermen were workers who transferred goods between ships and quays aboard flat-bottomed barges called lighters. Lightermen had their work cut out for them; a barge had a capacity of 500 tons, according to Wolf Bauer, the chief engineer.

This view shows the bow of the *Star of Chile*, tied up alongside the Roche Harbor wharf. With her three masts and prominent bowsprit, she was a proud sight in port or underway. H. E. Jamison, the noted *Seattle Star* reporter, wrote on October 14, 1935, that the *Star of Chile* had formerly been in the service of the Alaska Packers Association, the San Francisco–based manufacturer of Alaska canned salmon founded in 1891.

Two unidentified men pose for a photograph onboard the *Star of Chile*, Roche Harbor's schooner transport. She carried the logo "Roche Harbor Lime Transport" on her stern and lifeboats. Al Sundstrom was part of the crew that readied her for the U.S. Navy, which had purchased her for use as a barge. The navy took possession on December 6, 1941, the day before Pearl Harbor was attacked.

The *Archer*, left, was built at Sunderland, England, in 1876 as a 900-ton bark with a capacity of about 1,000 tons of general cargo. In 1894, she encountered a gale while en route from the Columbia River to Victoria, British Columbia; two crew members drowned. She was converted to a barkentine, and Roche Harbor bought her in September 1906 to join the *Irwin* in delivering lime to quake-ravaged San Francisco.

The *Archer* made history as the first commercial vessel on the West Coast fitted with wireless, but she had a tragic end. In 1915, she was chartered to take a lumber cargo to New York but put in to San Pedro, California, in distress. She was subsequently sold to Swayne and Hoyt, who installed an oil engine and operated her as the power schooner *Marie*. She wrecked off the Philippine Islands in 1936.

By 1915, the *Star of Chile* and a large iron freighter belonging to Roche Harbor were delivering nearly 100,000 barrels of lime a year along the Pacific Coast. "A good steam tug, about a dozen barges and two power launches" handled the bulk of the company's Puget Sound business, a company prospectus reported at the time.

Roche Harbor's shipyard, located north of the employees' cottages, maintained the company fleet of vessels. This area is located next to where the tennis courts are now; still visible at the site are rails and the boiler and propeller from the tug *Roche Harbor*.

John McMillin stands on the pier of his company town on July 23, 1923. This moment was the calm before the storm: On July 27, he photographed Pres. Warren G. and Florence Harding's visit to Seattle. On July 28, the buildings behind him went up in flames. On August 2, Harding died of a stroke in San Francisco. Roche Harbor interrupted rebuilding with a minute of silence in Harding's memory.

Roche Harbor had all the ingredients for disaster, specifically lime, which can be combustible depending on how it was processed, and wood, of which most of the buildings were comprised. On July 28, 1923, the lime plant and warehouse were razed by fire. John McMillin took this photograph, *Foundations at Kiln Battery No. 2, Roche Harbor Lime Works* with his No. 0 Graphic camera.

Roche Harbor shook off the devastation from the fire and immediately rebuilt on an expanded scale; kilns were in operation and the company was filling orders within three days. On September 1, the company hosted a party to thank employees and the community for helping to contain the fire. John McMillin conducted an "orchestra." "Musicians" performed using an anvil, cooper tools, a rock drill, and other tools of the trade.

Roche Harbor built a new store, offices, and warehouse after the fire. On the left, upstairs, is the Roche Harbor Community Hall and, with a water view, the Roche Harbor Yacht Club. The community hall and yacht club portions of the building, as well as the lime sheds, were demolished in 1970.

John McMillin promoted the agricultural, building, chemical, and plastering value of Roche Harbor's lime at the Puyallup Fair. McMillin boasted that his lime made apples redder, "marvelously increased" yields of grains and legumes, and was "the greatest" deodorizer and disinfectant. Dorothy Eckart Smith, daughter of Roche Harbor's secretary-treasurer John F. Eckart, wrote that McMillin gave away miniature lime barrels with the Roche Harbor logo.

The Tacoma Trading Company sold Roche Harbor lime, as well as building materials, coal, and Santa Cruz cement. The trading company drove this truck in parades throughout the Northwest to promote its products. The flag-bedecked, chain-driven rear-axle truck is carrying a well-organized display of Roche Harbor lime barrels.

Paul Hiett McMillin (1886–1961) spent his working life at Roche Harbor. He managed the company store and succeeded his brother as vice president in 1922 and his father as president in 1936. His job was no easy task. He managed the company during the Great Depression, changing markets, and labor unrest. In this portrait by Leonid Fink, the challenges of his job did not yet show in his demeanor. (Mary McMillin Cooper collection.)

Adda Morgan McMillin (1892–1959) helped her husband, Paul, run Roche Harbor after his father's death. She was born in Atlanta, Georgia, and graduated from Wesleyan College in Macon. She and Paul had a daughter, Mary; Paul had two daughters from an earlier marriage, Hope and Iva-Lou. (Mary McMillin Cooper collection.)

Roche Harbor was one of the last lime companies in the United States to unionize. Paul McMillin resisted, and in 1938, workers went on strike. McMillin was forced to give in when customers told him they could no longer buy "scab" lime. Ed Tuck is second from right, Gus Landahl third from right, Bill Mason fourth from right, and Art Fleming fifth from right. The strike lasted three months. (San Juan Historical Museum collection.)

Standing second from left, Wolf Bauer joined Roche Harbor's other salaried personnel in the quarries during the 1938 strike. An angry Paul McMillin met union representatives on the dock with a shotgun and announced that the company would operate without the workers. As union representatives watched, McMillin ordered Bauer to load spalls onto a waiting scow. The union representatives laughed, Bauer said; unionization was inevitable. (Wolf Bauer collection.)

Four

A COMMUNITY CALLED ROCHE HARBOR

Roche Harbor has been a company town and is now a boating resort, but for the people who have lived here over the centuries, it has been home.

At Roche Harbor from the 1880s on, family life continued much like it did at Whelaalk in the pre-settlement era. Couples met and fell in love here. Babies were born here. Children were raised and educated here.

Alexander Hall of Oswego, New York, came here to manage the cooperage department in 1893. He met Vela McCrary here, and they married in 1894. He taught their son, Vincent, the cooperage trade just as his father had taught him.

Angela Kreger and Ed Tuck grew up here, fell in love, and married in 1932, as did Caroline Chevalier and Norman Mills in 1937 and Mary McMillin and John Cooper in 1942.

Roche Harbor has always been a culturally diverse community. In John S. McMillin's day, a visitor might hear the dialect of Coast Salish people from both sides of the international border; the brogue of Irish-born Hughie Stoddert, an engineer in the 1890s; the Italian of the expert workers who had honed their skills in the quarries of their birth country; or the Japanese dialects of the cooks, gardeners, and powdermen.

As lime company president, McMillin could be a tough taskmaster. But his softer side came out here. He hosted his college buddies and Sigma Chi brothers. He was an avid boater, filmmaker, and photographer. He abstained from alcohol, leading business associates to nickname him "Lemonade Johnny."

He and his wife, the former Louella Hiett (1857–1943), had been childhood sweethearts in Sugar Grove, Indiana. She graduated from Ohio Wesleyan University. She served as Roche Harbor's postmaster from 1892 to 1940 and taught Sunday school. A 1910 *Bellingham Herald* biography of her husband referred to her as "coadjutor in the promotion of the educational, moral and civic conditions which have made Roche Harbor the ideal industrial center it is today."

She was also humble. Despite her own accomplishments, her tombstone reads simply, "Wife of John S. McMillin."

Together, John and Louella McMillin had four children: John Hiett, who died in infancy; Fred Hiett, born in 1880; Paul Hiett, born in 1886; and Dorothy Hiett, born in 1894. They also had four granddaughters: Fred's daughter Evelyn, and Paul's daughters Hope, Iva-Lou, and Mary.

John and Louella McMillin were married on June 5, 1877. Fifty years later, John would write of their life together, "Fifty years we've planned and wrought, Louella Dear; / Sharing every joy and sorrow, smile and tear. / Toil together lighter grew, Burdens less when borne by two / Joys more sweet when shared with you, Louella Dear." They would have four children and four granddaughters.

Fred Hiett McMillin (1880–1922) and Paul Hiett McMillin (1886–1961), sons of John S. and Louella Hiett McMillin, pursued careers at the company their father founded. Dorothy Hiett McMillin (1894–1980) was described as lively and pretty. She attended the University of Washington, but her emotional condition changed. In her youth, she had a nanny, Adah Beeny. In her senior years, her niece Mary helped care for her. (Mary McMillin Cooper collection.)

Louella McMillin's parents were John and Mary Hiett of Sugar Grove, Indiana. John Hiett (1808–1895), like his son-in-law's father, John King McMillin, was a farmer and stock raiser of some affluence. Mary Hiett (1824–1910) died at Roche Harbor in October 1910. (Mary McMillin Cooper collection.)

A boy rides his horse on the dirt road in front of the Hotel de Haro in the early 1890s. Mary McMillin Cooper, a granddaughter of John and Louella McMillin, said the boy could be her father, Paul. The hotel is believed to have been built on the site of the Scurr brothers' bunkhouse, with some of the timbers used in the bunkhouse construction visible today. (Mary McMillin Cooper collection.)

Another early view of the Hotel de Haro reveals early kilns, the warehouse, and the sunken area that would become the gardens. The kilns closest to the hotel are vertical draw kilns, in which limestone is fed into the top of the kiln and cooked by fireplaces located at the sides, and resemble those that came into widespread use in limestone manufacture in the 1860s.

The Hotel de Haro, pictured around 1890, served many functions. New employees and visitors stayed there. Employees dined there. And until 1910, John and Louella McMillin lived there. Today the hotel is still the centerpiece of a growing community. The two boys to the left of the men in aprons are likely Fred and Paul McMillin. (Mary McMillin Cooper collection.)

John McMillin stands at left with guests on a Hotel de Haro balcony around 1890. Within 10 years, the town of Roche Harbor would be described as having a "warehouse, a large general store, a fine commodious wharf, a magnificent hotel—the Hotel de Haro—a church and schoolhouse, barns and a large number of private residences, all neatly painted and kept in the best condition."

A couple relaxes in Room 3A of the Hotel de Haro in 1900. Victorian-era appointments included a sideboard and hutch; leather, wicker, and needlepoint chairs; china; and a silver tea set. In the far right corner is a writing desk. This room also contained a piano. Some house rules were unusual: nurses were not allowed in the laundry, and the tab had to be paid the evening before departure.

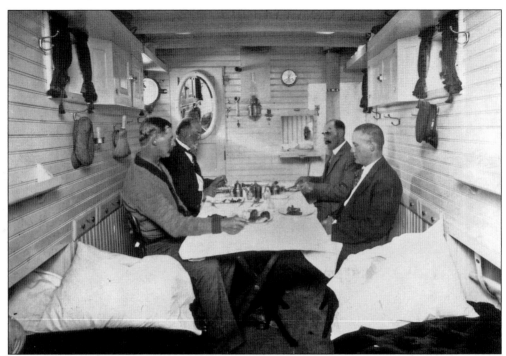

John McMillin hosted his friend, Robert Pim Butchart, on a cruise aboard the *Calcite* from September 9 to 25, 1908. McMillin's 50-foot yacht cruised as far north as Princess Louisa Inlet. Enjoying lunch are, clockwise from front left to right, first officer Henry Horst, McMillin, Butchart, and McMillin's oldest son, Fred. Chief steward Jim Nagaoka looks in from the galley window. Butchart's own lime quarry in Victoria, British Columbia, would become Butchart Gardens.

Another *Calcite* passenger was photographer John A. McCormick, who documented the adventure with his camera and log. Over 17 days, the group explored, fished, and hunted. McCormick took this photograph of the *Calcite* on her return to Roche Harbor, moored at Fred McMillin's boathouse. Bearskins and other hides are displayed on the bow. John McMillin stands next to the pilothouse. One of the bearskins was displayed in McMillin's office.

John McCormick captured a lot of early-20th-century Friday Harbor and Roche Harbor with his camera. With this creative New Year's Day greeting card, he wished his clients and friends a prosperous 1916. "Nothing that I can do or make or buy will, in any sense, express the great happiness I wish you during the year 1916," he wrote. (Capron family collection.)

Shigeru "Bill" Nagaoka (1906–1994) and his father, Sukeichi "Jim" Nagaoka, the McMillins' chief steward, are pictured here. "He was never at a loss for something new in pastry or pudding and was continually giving us the last word in delicious compounds from his three-by-five-foot galley," John McCormick wrote of Nagaoka. The Nagaoka home was near the barrel factory, looking toward Pearl Pass. (Nagaoka family collection.)

Pictured here are Bill Nagaoka and his mother, Kaju Sagawa Nagaoka. Many Japanese families counted the McMillins as friends. Mary McMillin Cooper, a granddaughter of John and Louella McMillin, remembers receiving a crate of cantaloupes each season from families that had moved to eastern Washington to farm. (Nagaoka family collection.)

Bill Nagaoka is at far left with four unidentified children in Roche Harbor. The Nagaokas stayed a couple of nights with Paul and Adda McMillin shortly before the McMillins sold Roche Harbor in 1956. An employee took the Nagaoka's son, Dick, fishing in Pearl Pass and let him take an item from the company store. He chose a wooden fishing plug for a memento. (Nagaoka family collection.)

58

Mary Frances Hiett's last year of life was spent in the celebration and company of family in Roche Harbor. Her children and grandchildren dance around her birthday cake on July 9, 1910, in the Hotel de Haro banquet court in celebration of her 86th birthday. This day was a landmark day for her, as the next photograph attests.

Mary Hiett's 86th birthday coincided with the christening of her great-granddaughter, Hope Grant McMillin, the daughter of Paul and Iva Grant McMillin. Hope was christened by her granduncles, the Reverend W. B. McMillin and the Reverend William Switzer. Reverend McMillin was John McMillin's brother. Reverend Switzer was married to Louella McMillin's sister, Anna. Mrs. Hiett died in October that year.

Ruth Youngberg's parents, Edward and Angela "Peg" Tuck, started their lives as a married couple in Roche Harbor. Youngberg said these tidy employee cottages were served by a community well and had their own outhouses and many, like her parents', had vegetable gardens. The Tarte family redeveloped this site beginning in 1957 and installed a pool, tennis courts, and a sweeping lawn. The nine remaining cottages are now rented to resort guests.

Ed Tuck and his wife, the former Angela Kreger, stand next to their 1929 Ford Roadster. They were entrenched in Roche Harbor life. She was born here, as were two of her five children. Her father worked here. Ed crushed rock, fired the kilns, worked in the power plant, and became an assistant foreman. Their garden helped supply their table during the strike in 1938. (Joyce Lowe collection.)

John McMillin, a devoted Methodist, had this church built at Roche Harbor by 1889; it served as a school during the week. In this *c.* 1933 photograph is Gwendolyn Martin, standing at front center with short dark hair and bow; her uncles, Stan Rouleau and Wilfred Rouleau, worked for Roche Harbor. To her left is Shiz Yasuda, whose dad was a gardener and whose mother was a cook.

From left to right, Matsuko, Haru, Kay, Suzie, and Kendo Yasuda pose in front of their home in the section of Roche Harbor known by its residents as Japan Town. Immigrant Japanese people and their children were an important part of Roche Harbor life from the 1890s to the 1940s. The children attended the village school, and their family counted the McMillins as friends. (Shimizu family collection.)

Machinist's Mate William Chevalier of the U.S. Navy was one of 10 young Roche Harbor and Stuart Island men to serve in World War I. Others were Pvt. Henry John Balam, U.S. Army; 1st Cook Henry C. Balch, U.S. Army; Electrical Sgt. 1st Class Clarence Bell, U.S. Army; Oiler Instructor Lawrence Borchers, U.S. Navy; Machinist 1st Class Louis Borchers Jr., U.S. Navy; Sgt. Walter Butterworth, U.S. Marine Corps; Fireman 1st Class Harold Butterworth, U.S. Navy; Pvt. Alexander Hall, U.S. Army; and Gun Capt. George Franklin Scribner, U.S. Navy. Harold Butterworth died of pneumonia at the naval hospital in Brooklyn, New York; his name is included on a monument in Memorial Park in Friday Harbor. (Wilma Rimer collection.)

John McMillin carves at a dinner for 11 male guests in the Hotel de Haro dining room at Christmas 1912 as a staff of five attendants stands by. The table is lavishly decorated with madrona leaves, berries, and grapes. McMillin enjoyed holiday traditions and had some of his own. Granddaughter Mary McMillin Cooper said he picked a bouquet from the hotel gardens for his wife every New Year's Day.

Guests board Roche Harbor's festival barge for transport to an event on Henry Island's McCracken Point, which was owned by the company. Salmon barbecues "were held on points and islets in the vicinity, and barges imaginatively decked with evergreens . . . were used to tow guests forth and back," wrote Elisabeth Walton Potter in Roche Harbor's nomination for the National Register of Historic Places in 1976.

John McMillin's yacht, the *Calcite*, and the company tug *Roche Harbor* towed the festival barge to McCracken Point, one of the venues for Roche Harbor's annual Harvest Festival. "Guests were treated to salmon and corn cooked in the beach gravel, Indian style," according to a photograph donated to the San Juan Historical Museum by Jack and Vaunita McMurray.

Guests enjoy the beach at the August 1920 Harvest Festival. Rosella Herdt leans on the rock in the foreground. On the grass, from left to right, are Bill Rogers, William Chevalier, Ethel Martin, Stan Rouleau, John Rogers, Bessie Baty, Violet Rouleau, Hazel Baty, Minnie Raybell, Alfred Chevalier, and Iva-Lou McMillin (Paul McMillin's daughter). Frank Rouleau kneels at right wearing a hat. John and Louella McMillin are on the barge at center. (San Juan Historical Museum collection.)

Frank Rouleau, wearing a hat, is on the far right on the festival barge in August 1920. Third and fourth from right are Mary Crook Davis, whose husband Herbert H. Davis was a retired boat captain for Roche Harbor, and her brother, Jim Crook, who was farming the homestead on the former British military camp. (Neil Tarte collection.)

An unidentified man holds a prize catch during an outing at Roche Harbor. Abundant salmon runs thrilled visitors, stocked company larders, and supplemented local tables. During lean times in the 1930s and 1940s, Ed and Peg Tuck of Roche Harbor clammed, fished, and canned or smoked 14- to 16-pound chum salmon they bought from local reef-netters for 25¢.

Roche Harbor was a bustling industrial town, but its gardens, hotel, pavilion, and harbor views made a lovely setting for the wedding of Wesley McCrary and Ethel Buchanan, both of San Juan Island. They married on March 28, 1925, in a quadruple wedding ceremony held in the Roche Harbor Community Hall above the store. Roche Harbor is still a popular wedding venue.

John McMillin was an avid yachtsman who in 1906 founded the Roche Harbor Yacht Club, which met in this room above the store. The club was active until 1942 and was reactivated in 1957. Based on a review of club records, Reuben J. Tarte wrote, "there were two excellent club rooms, one with a maple dance floor and stage, the other a projection room and a billiard table."

The former British military camp, settled by the Crook family after troops left in 1872, was a popular attraction for the McMillins' guests. This group poses in front of the blockhouse. In August 1932, a reporter wrote of Harvest Festival guests being entertained by visits to American and English camps after an open-air banquet with live music.

John McMillin's employees and guests enjoyed eggs and poultry from his Bellevue Poultry Farm on Westcott Bay, near what is now the entrance to Roche Harbor Village, as well as beef and lamb from W. H. McCrary's 186-acre farm nearby. Among the breeds of fowl raised at Bellevue were Crystal White Orpingtons, developed in England in 1886, the same year the Hotel de Haro was built.

A kitchen crew prepares salmon for a gathering. The abundant salmon runs in the area, as well as poultry and other meats from Roche Harbor's Bellevue Farm, helped stock the company's larders. The label on the box at right refers to "bleached cheesecloth," which is used in kitchens for basting and poaching as well as straining soups and sauces.

Roche Harbor's chefs were skilled as well as creative; this presentation was called "a king salmon battleship ready for action." Life at Roche Harbor "was enlivened from time to time by the entertainments on which McMillin seemed to pride himself," historic preservation specialist Elisabeth Walton Potter wrote in 1976.

A crowd enjoys patriotic music from a band in front of the Hotel de Haro on July 4, 1925. This celebration was likely an all-day affair; other photographs of the day show guests enjoying dinner on the banquet court.

Chefs prepare salmon near the banquet court fireplace on July 4, 1925. The banquet court was a popular venue for entertaining; it could be covered in inclement weather and uncovered when sunny. Music was often performed in the hotel for guests' entertainment. The woman in the middle, facing the camera, is Ichi Yasuda, who worked as a cook and gardener for the McMillins. She rowed from her home to the McMillins' daily.

A larger soiree hosted by the McMillins in the Hotel de Haro banquet court is pictured here. The lime and cement company's success, combined with its prolific poultry farm and healthy salmon runs in Mosquito Pass, enabled the McMillins to entertain lavishly. John McMillin is seated at center in the rear. To his left, with a goatee, is his college chum Judge Caleb S. Denny of Indianapolis, Indiana.

The Hotel de Haro banquet court was the venue for the Roche Harbor Harvest Festival on August 1, 1926. John McMillin installed a limestone fireplace in the court, above which is written "Friendship's fires are always burning." The court, fireplace, and motto are still there. Roche Harbor hosted a Harvest Festival every August for at least 35 years.

John McMillin coaches a class of Sigma Chi pledges at Purdue University in West Lafayette, Indiana, on November 18, 1930. McMillin was Sigma Chi's first grand consul, or international president, and remained active in fraternity affairs throughout his adult life. He installed chapters at several universities, among them are Washington State University and the University of Oregon, and donated the limestone for the Sigma Chi house at University of Washington.

John McMillin was widely known for his business and political interests, but there was a softer side to the one-time Senate hopeful—he was an avid photographer, amateur filmmaker, and writer. In January 1930, he penned this tribute to Mount Baker, known in the Nooksack language as "Kulshan." (Mary McMillin Cooper collection.)

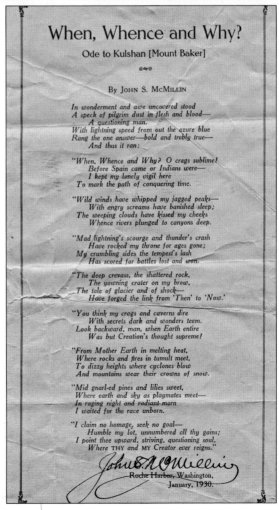

When, Whence and Why?

Ode to Kulshan [Mount Baker]

By John S. McMillin

In wonderment and awe uncovered stood
A speck of pilgrim dust in flesh and blood—
*   A questioning man.*
With lightning speed from out the azure blue
Rang the one answer—bold and trebly true—
*   And thus it ran:*

"When, Whence and Why? O crags sublime!
*   Before Spain came or Indians were—*
I kept my lonely vigil here
*   To mark the path of conquering time.*

"Wild winds have whipped my jagged peaks—
*   With angry screams have banished sleep;*
The weeping clouds have kissed my cheeks
*   Whence rivers plunged to canyons deep.*

"Mad lightning's scourge and thunder's crash
*   Have rocked my throne for ages gone;*
My crumbling sides the tempest's lash
*   Has scored for battles lost and won.*

"The deep crevass, the shattered rock,
*   The yawning crater on my brow,*
The tale of glacier and of shock—
*   Have forged the link from 'Then' to 'Now.'*

"You think my crags and caverns dire
*   With secrets dark and wonders teem.*
Look backward, man, when Earth entire
*   Was but Creation's thought supreme!*

"From Mother Earth in melting heat,
Where rocks and fires in tumult meet,
To dizzy heights where cyclones blow
And mountains wear their crowns of snow.

"Mid gnarl-ed pines and lilies sweet,
*   Where earth and sky as playmates meet—*
In raging night and radiant morn
I waited for the race unborn.

"I claim no homage, seek no goal—
*   Humble my lot, unnumbered all thy gains;*
I point thee upward, striving, questioning soul,
*   Where THY and MY Creator ever reigns."*

John S. McMillin
Roche Harbor, Washington,
January, 1930.

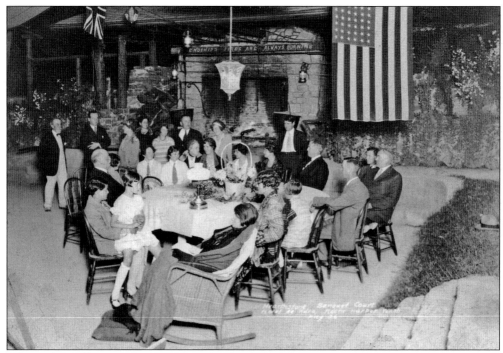

John and Louella McMillin entertain friends on the banquet court in August 1926. John is the older gentleman seated at left; Louella is seated at middle left, wearing a black neckband. Dorothy Eckart Smith, whose father held various white-collar positions with the company, shares the chair at front. A dog naps at the feet of the woman in the rocking chair.

At the Turkey Shoot Banquet on January 15, 1925, guests paid 25¢ each for a shot at a target; the closest shot won a turkey. John and Louella McMillin are seated at left; Paul McMillin is standing next to the wall at center right. Wesley McCrary and Ethel Buchanan, engaged to be married on March 28, 1925, are seated at right next to the man with the baby. Seated at Buchanan's right is Adah Beeny, the McMillins' nanny and family companion. (Neil Tarte collection.)

Heisaku and Ichi Yasuda visited Roche Harbor around 1950 with one of their sons, George, and their youngest daughter, Sue. They hold two octopuses they had caught. "Octopus is a delicacy and is eaten during New Year's," Yasuda in-law Cho Shimizu wrote. "Another delicacy was the Matsutake mushrooms, which were plentiful on Roche Harbor. They are known as pine mushrooms." (Shimizu family collection.)

Louella McMillin (holding a basket), her daughter Dorothy, and visitors pose for a photograph under a farewell greeting on the trellised path leading from the hotel to the harbor. Visitors to Roche Harbor today walk below the farewell "Adieu."

John McMillin, standing, entertains guests at a broiled king salmon banquet in August 1926 on the Hotel de Haro banquet court. Under the canopy hang Chinese lanterns and British, Canadian, and U.S. flags. Visible at right is a photograph display titled "Kodaking Roche Harbor;" at center is an organ used to entertain guests. The organ is a fixture in the hotel lobby today.

Masonic lodge members and their spouses disembark from the ferry *Kalakala* around 1935 for a McMillin salmon bake on Pearl Island. "The Masons were having a big do in Seattle," said Mary McMillin Cooper, Paul McMillin's daughter. "The *Kalakala* brought them up to Pearl Island for a salmon bake. The salmon was prepared Indian style."

John Stafford McMillin and Louella Hiett McMillin had these portraits taken on the occasion of their 50th wedding anniversary, June 5, 1927. In an anniversary book, the couple honored each other with poems; Louella chose a Robert Burns poem: "John Anderson my joy, John, We climbed the hill together / And many a jolly day, John, We have had with one another." (Mary McMillin Cooper collection.)

In the anniversary book, John McMillin paid tribute to his wife with a poem that, in part, read, "They say we're growing old, Louella Dear, And chiming bells tell of another year / But our hearts are just as young as when happy bells were rung." (Mary McMillin Cooper collection.)

John and Louella McMillin relax at home on what is described in a Roche Harbor Village brochure as their "semicircular deck which was covered by a conical striped canopy which in good weather enabled Mr. and Mrs. McMillin to overlook their formal gardens and the bustling activity of the harbor." The home was built about 1910; until then, the McMillins lived in the Hotel de Haro.

The interior of John and Louella McMillin's home was comfortable, well built, and well furnished, but not ostentatious, said granddaughter Mary McMillin Cooper. A painting of the church and school is displayed on a chair. This area of the elder McMillins' home is part of the modern restaurant but is recognizable.

Afterglow Mansion, built by Fred McMillin in 1910, overlooked Speiden Channel. It was named for the rosy light that appears in the sky after sunset. After Fred died in 1922, his parents spent time in the home. It was destroyed by fire in the 1940s. Among the items destroyed in the fire was a closet full of home movies made by John McMillin. (Mary McMillin Cooper collection.)

John McMillin poses in the garden of Afterglow Manor. The stone building under construction in the background was built by the elder McMillin as a Sigma Chi fraternity retreat, according to granddaughter Mary McMillin Cooper.

Paul McMillin waits on the dock at Roche Harbor as his daughter, Mary, and her classmates and teachers from St. Margaret's School arrive via a chartered boat from Oak Bay, British Columbia, in the spring of 1936. St. Margaret's School is the oldest continuous private day and boarding school on Vancouver Island. (Mary McMillin Cooper collection.)

Mary McMillin, her classmates, and teachers from St. Margaret's School enjoy a luncheon on the Hotel de Haro banquet court, the scene of so many similar earlier gatherings; by 1936, such gatherings were rare. Wolf Bauer, the chief engineer, said 1936 was "a time that saw the last of lavish parties and dances in the sunken gardens at the Hotel de Haro." (Mary McMillin Cooper collection.)

Paul McMillin's stern expression belies his enjoyment of being out on the water. This picture captures the avid boater on a family outing onboard the *Mary Adda*. From left to right are an unidentified woman, Adda McMillin, Mary McMillin, and Paul McMillin. In 1936, he succeeded his father as company president and was an alternate delegate to the Republican National Convention. (Mary McMillin Cooper collection.)

Mary McMillin Cooper poses in a Mexican dress and headpiece presented to her by family friends around 1936. She maintained a regular correspondence with her grandmother, whom she called "Momo," while studying at St. Margaret's School. Mary named one of her sons Hiett—her grandmother's maiden name—in her grandmother's honor. (Mary McMillin Cooper collection.)

This is a view of John and Louella McMillin's waterfront home, with the Hotel de Haro on the higher elevation at right. Fifty years after her parents sold Roche Harbor, Mary McMillin Cooper fondly remembered the village of her youth as a reporter described it in August 1932: "Whitewashed and friendly. . . . The whole town sparkles with neatness." (Mary McMillin Cooper collection.)

Heisaku Yasuda tends the lawn at the hotel gardens around 1926. Yasuda was a powder man and gardener as well as a midwife. Louella McMillin taught his wife, Ichi, how to make barbecue, spaghetti, turkey stuffing, stir fry, and desserts. The family later moved to Wapato, but decades later, "Mrs. McMillin's turkey stuffing is still a favorite at their Thanksgiving dinners," Cho Shimizu wrote in 2008.

Five

A Doctor in the House

Just as John S. McMillin employed business acumen and moxie to build Tacoma and Roche Harbor Lime Company, Victor James Capron's boundless energy and ingenuity propelled him from company doctor to island doctor to legislator.

Capron (1867–1934) was born in Rome, New York, and graduated from Jefferson Medical College in Philadelphia in 1888. He was resident physician of St. Luke's Hospital in South Bethlehem, Pennsylvania, and surgeon of the Norwegian Deaconess Home and Hospital in Brooklyn, New York.

In 1893, he became government physician in Kau, Hawaii, arriving in Honolulu on March 10, 1893. He employed a rigid quarantine to contain a cholera epidemic in 1895.

In March 1898, Capron became Roche Harbor's doctor; by 1901, he was seeing patients one day a week in Friday Harbor as well. He founded the island's telephone system; Etta Egeland (1896–2002) said her aunt, Nellie Flinn, had one of the first telephones. "She was kind of an informer. . . . If there was any medical trouble that came up, she would notify Dr. Capron."

Capron founded a hospital at Argyle Avenue and Spring Street in Friday Harbor and delivered more than 500 island babies. He developed a way to power an X-ray machine with his automobile so that he could determine the extent of injuries at the scene of a medical call.

Capron was as daring as he was ingenious. Once, while driving in a storm, he saw a telephone wire that had been broken in a gale. He climbed up a tree and put the wire back together.

Capron was an equally indefatigable legislator: he served on the Friday Harbor Town Council, (1911–1912); was mayor (1912–1914; 1930–1932) and state representative (1913–1917; 1923–1927); and sat on the state board of health (1919–1934).

As mayor, he acquired Trout Lake for the town's water supply. As state representative, he wrote legislation that gives ferry-dependent communities a share of state gas tax revenue for use in improving and maintaining local roads. There are no state roads in the San Juans. The fund represents money that would be spent here if there were.

"There was nothing too difficult for Dr. Capron," Egeland said.

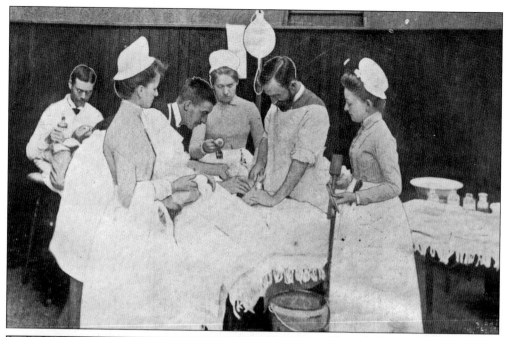

Victor J. Capron, at left, administers anesthesia during a surgery at St. Luke's Hospital in South Bethlehem, Pennsylvania, in 1890. Three years later, he left the states for Hawaii to become government physician in Kau district. (Capron family collection.)

From left to right are Tom Delaney and Victor J. Capron, in Naalehu, Kau, Hawaii, in July 1893. During a cholera epidemic in 1895, Capron maintained a rigid quarantine to keep the disease out of Kau. On August 31, 1895, the *Honolulu Advertiser* opined that a cholera bacillus "would probably starve to death for want of filth of any kind, owing to the efficient work of Dr. Capron, et al." (Capron family collection.)

Roche Harbor's company store probably looked like this when Dr. Capron arrived in 1898. A customer could buy hardware, paint, a kerosene lamp, and a wood stove, as well as groceries and other household goods. The store's manager then was Thomas R. Kinsey, a native of Shropshire, England. This store, at the end of the wharf, burned in 1923 and was replaced by the current store. (Capron family collection.)

Workers received coupon books redeemable at the company store in lieu of cash. This book from the 1930s was worth $2 and contained coupons worth 10¢, 5¢, 2¢, and 1¢. Workers could get paid in cash if requested, an increasing necessity as Roche Harbor attracted seasonal and permanent workers who lived outside the village.

The street in front of the Hotel de Haro takes on a festive flair during an event in the early 1900s. The hotel's proximity to the limekilns is clear in this photograph. Clearly visible is the rail line leading to the chutes, which funneled limestone into the kilns below. These two kilns have been preserved and are part of the modern landscape. (Capron family collection.)

Dr. Capron lived in this once-fine Victorian home at Roche Harbor after he arrived in 1898 and then used it as a Roche Harbor medical office after he moved to Friday Harbor. It was later used for employee housing by the lime company and the resort but ultimately fell into disrepair. It was torn down in 2004 to make way for a new neighborhood of 1900s-style homes.

Peter Kirk (1840–1916) was Dr. Capron's father-in-law and had homes at Mitchell Bay and Friday Harbor. Kirk, an English-born steelmaker, established the town of Kirkland on Lake Washington with the intent of building a steel mill there. He had Roche Harbor's lime tested for purity for use as a flux. His mill never materialized, thanks in part to the economic depression of 1893. (Capron family collection.)

Mary Ann Quirk Kirk (1849–1907) was born on the Isle of Man, the daughter of a prosperous sail maker. She and Peter Kirk married in the 1860s and immigrated to Washington territory in 1887. She shared her love of music with her daughters and made sure they were well educated. After her death, her husband "spent many long days in retirement with his solitude and his music." (Capron family collection.)

Victor and Fanny Kirk Capron are pictured with their children, Marjorie and Victor Jr. Fanny Valentine Kirk Capron (1875–1956) played the violin, wrote some musical compositions, helped raise her sister Marie's children after Marie's death in 1904, and volunteered in the community. (Capron family collection.)

The Capron family relaxes at their home, today known as Kirk House, a bed and breakfast. From left to right are possibly Vivian or Charlotte Bell, a niece; Marjorie, the Caprons' daughter, born in 1903; an unidentified woman; Dr. Victor Capron; an unidentified man; Mrs. Fanny Capron and her son, Victor Jr. (Capron family collection.)

Victor Capron Jr. (1908–1986), the son of the doctor, prepares a meal at his beach camp around 1941. Several islanders had waterfront lots as weekend getaways, complete with old wood-burning stoves that they hauled to the beach. He had an auto dealership and garage on the corner of Spring Street and Argyle Avenue. He served on the Friday Harbor Town Council from 1934 to 1941. (Capron family collection.)

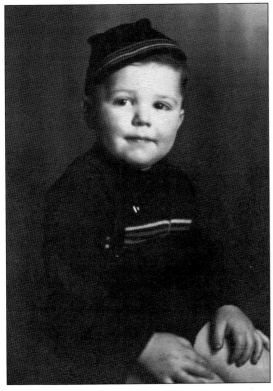

Victor J. Capron III, the doctor's grandson, was born on December 29, 1934, to Victor Capron Jr. and Ruth Jakle. Ruth's parents, William and Sophie Heidenreich Jakle, farmed on Mount Finlayson near the former American military camp. The younger Capron became a prominent fisherman and a collector of local artifacts. He served on the Friday Harbor Town Council from 1976 to 1979 and on the San Juan County Marine Resources Committee. (Capron family collection.)

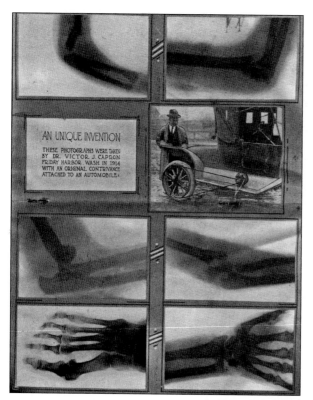

San Juan Island, in an isolated northwest county, was fortunate to have an innovative doctor like Victor J. Capron as one of its residents. He developed a way to power his X-ray machine with his automobile so he could better determine the extent of injuries at the scene of the call. He also wrote a book on birthing and infant care. (Capron family collection.)

State Representative Victor J. Capron, who was also serving as mayor, is depicted in this cartoon on the front page of the November 27, 1913, *Friday Harbor Journal*. An elephant, the symbol of the Republican Party, carries what appears to be his medical kit. The map in Capron's hand refers to a road that would be built leading from town to the University of Washington marine research station. (Capron family collection.)

REPRESENTATIVE V. J. CAPRON OF SAN JUAN COUNTY
As the cartoonist saw him at Olympia, while attending the 1913 session of the Legislature.

Representative Capron ran for the Washington State Senate in 1916, hoping to represent the 24th District, then composed of Clallam, Jefferson, and San Juan Counties. A card promoting his candidacy told of his varied abilities; the doctor/legislator managed to find time to raise oats and peas, operate a dairy, and run 1,000 sheep. The election, however, was won by A. A. Smith of Clallam County. (Capron family collection.)

VICTOR J. CAPRON
FRIDAY HARBOR, WASHINGTON
Republican Candidate for State Senator, 24th District
Comprising Jefferson, Clallam and San Juan Counties
[OVER]

VICTOR J. CAPRON,

Candidate for the nomination for State Senator on the Republican ticket, was born on a farm in Oneida county, New York, was raised under a "holy" straw hat with his "feet on the ground"; served as government Physician in Hawaii three years; was a member of the Washington legislature in 1913 and 1915, and was a member of the Rural Credits Commission (farm loans).

Dr. Capron owns 2140 acres on San Juan Island and this year has 200 acres in peas and 40 in oats; operated a dairy and runs about 1000 sheep. This is mentioned to assure the farmers that their interests and his are the same. All other interests and enterprises would receive his loyal support and service.

Dr. Capron sits at his desk in the Washington State House of Representatives in Olympia. He served on the following committees: Agriculture; Appropriations; Dairy and Livestock; Industrial Insurance; Medicine, Surgery, Dentistry, and Hygiene; Fisheries; Memorials; and State School and Granted Lands. Constituents seeking his help included John S. McMillin, who on February 23, 1915, asked for support for a bill that would allow farmers to grow certain game birds. (Capron family collection.)

Dr. Capron was encouraged to run for Washington State Senate again in 1918 by a group of ladies clubs in Port Angeles, who felt that the other two candidates, including the incumbent, William Bishop, "have in the past favored the liquor interests." In 1919, Capron became a member of the Washington State Board of Health and then returned to the Washington State House of Representatives from 1923 to 1927. (Capron family collection.)

Port angeles Wash Aug 4: 1918

Dr Capron
    Friday Harbor Wash

Dear Doctor
    By request of our Ladys clubs I was apointed and asked to write you and ask you if you had filed for Senator of our dist we do hope you will as we want to give you our Soport as we know that both Mr Bishop and Mr Fisher have in the past favored the Liquor intrests and we would rather vote for a man like you that we can depend on with both Bishop and Fisher being candidates and any from your County we feel sure of your Election let us know as soon as possible by return mail.
    your Friend
    Mrs Fitzgerald
    Box 276
    Port Angeles Wash

Six

CHARACTERS, LEGENDS, AND LORE

Roche Harbor's breathtaking beauty and rich natural resources have long attracted dreamers and visionaries.

John Stafford McMillin (1855–1936) was arguably Roche Harbor's first "character." He was postmaster of Roche Harbor from 1887 to 1892, a U.S. Senate candidate in 1895, founder of the Roche Harbor Yacht Club in 1906, a member of the state utilities commission from 1906 to 1908, and a Republican National Convention delegate in 1924 and 1932. But he was by no means the only prominent political figure to grace the village.

Hugh Campbell Wallace (1863–1931) was involved in the early development of Tacoma and was an early investor in Tacoma and Roche Harbor Lime Company; his brother, Thomas, was on the company's board of trustees. Hugh Wallace was a partner in a Tacoma smelter, and in Roche Harbor, he had a ready supply of lime for use in making steel. The Wallaces testified in favor of McMillin in a lawsuit filed by McMillin's competitor, Henry Cowell.

In 1891, Hugh Wallace married the daughter of U.S. Chief Justice Melville Fuller. He served on the Democratic National Committee from 1892 to 1896, and in 1897, he organized a steamship line from Tacoma to Alaska. Wallace returned to the Democratic National Committee in 1916 and served as U.S. ambassador to France from 1919 to 1921.

Wolf Bauer, born in 1912, launched a distinguished engineering career at Roche Harbor in 1936, shortly after graduating from University of Washington. He became equally distinguished for his contributions to conservation, kayaking, mountain rescue, and skiing. He founded the Washington Kayak Club and helped popularize kayaking in the Pacific Northwest.

Actor John Wayne (1907–1979), an avid yachtsman, made Roche Harbor the summer homeport for his converted minesweeper, the *Wild Goose*, in the 1960s and 1970s.

Roche Harbor contributed scenery and talent to the 1966 film *Namu, the Killer Whale*. Resort co-owner Clara Tarte was "discovered" while tending to her garden and was cast as Carrie, a gun-toting villager who protests a marine biologist's protection of a killer whale. Her grandson, Neil Tarte Jr., also had a part in the film.

Einar Nielsen (1932–1984) built roads for Roche Harbor Resort, became the resort's vice president, and served on the San Juan County Commission from 1978 to 1979. He was an avid fisherman and died of an apparent heart attack while fishing. He was found on his boat with a 50-pound salmon—the largest salmon he had ever caught. The Einar Nielsen/Becky Barr Memorial Fishing Classic in September is named in his memory.

Capt. James W. Tarte, uncle of Roche Harbor Resort founder Reuben J. Tarte, was skipper of the steamers *Evangel* and *Brick* in the 1880s, delivering mail and passengers between Bellingham, Victoria, Port Angeles, and points between. Captain Tarte stands on the railing at right. It was likely Tarte who, on June 4, 1883, took Philip Clayton Van Buskirk to Roche Harbor in the sailor and diarist's first of several unsuccessful attempts to homestead an island in the area.

John S. McMillin was influential in business and politics, and he wanted young people to have opportunities to succeed in those fields too. He was devoted to Sigma Chi and its mission of developing leaders committed to friendship, justice, and learning. And in 1935, he allowed a new summer camp for children to use land on Westcott Bay for $1 a year for 10 years; the camp is now Camp Nor'wester on Johns Island.

John McMillin's two avocations, photography and politics, come together in these startling photographs. McMillin photographed Pres. Warren G. and Florence Harding's visit to Seattle on July 27, 1923, using a No. 0 Graphic film-roll camera. Harding waves from his car as he arrives at University of Washington Stadium. The Seattle speech was Harding's last; he died of a stroke in San Francisco six days later.

The USS *Henderson* arrives at Bell Street dock in Seattle with President and Mrs. Harding onboard; a captain's gig is pulling alongside to receive the first couple and bring them ashore. Harding visited Alaska; Vancouver, British Columbia; Washington; Oregon; and California in a "Voyage of Understanding" to meet residents of the West and talk to them about his policies. When he died on August 2, Roche Harbor observed a minute of silence.

Clifford K. McMillin (1877–1957), a nephew of John S. McMillin, had become vice president of Northwestern National Bank in Bellingham when this portrait was taken in 1906. He and his parents, Methodist minister William B. and Arietta McMillin, came to Puget Sound in 1883 and settled in Bellingham in 1892. In his career, Clifford also served as a cannery president, school board member, and port commissioner. (Anne Guthrie collection.)

Cliff McMillin, now known as the "fishing realtor," displays a prize catch. His boat was called the *See Cliff* because if one wanted to learn about real estate in the San Juans, one would "See Cliff." Broadcast journalist Edward R. Murrow caught two 25-pound salmon on an outing in 1946. McMillin described Murrow as "as common as an old shoe and as friendly as can be." (Anne Guthrie collection.)

Hugh Campbell Wallace, U.S. ambassador to France (1917–1921), was born in Missouri and in 1887 settled in Tacoma, where he engaged in the real estate business with his brother, Thomas. Among his investments was Tacoma and Roche Harbor Lime Company. He had a personality that "enabled him to associate on equal terms with prominent people everywhere," according to a contemporary biography. He became prominent in business, politics, and diplomacy. (Hugh C. Wallace collection.)

John McMillin poses with some college buddies on July 31, 1922, at the Hotel de Haro. From left to right are Judge Caleb S. Denny of Indianapolis, Judge Howard Ferris of Cincinnati, Judge John C. McClain of Salt Lake City, and McMillin. Denny served as mayor of Indianapolis from 1886 to 1890 and from 1893 to 1895 and as a presidential elector in 1908. McClain was a delegate to the Republican National Convention in 1908.

Roche Harbor captain Herbert H. Davis (1867–1929) and his wife, Mary Crook, were married in 1897. In 1920, he opened H. H. Davis Lumber in Friday Harbor and served as mayor there from 1923 to 1926. Other Roche Harbor employees who became public servants include William Shultz, company superintendent, who served in the state house of representatives from 1905–1909, and Hubert L. Cahail, bus driver and wood splitter, who served as Friday Harbor mayor from 1942 to 1948. (Town of Friday Harbor.)

Scottish-born Dolina Nellis Houde bought the Scurr brothers' former home on White Point and operated a sheep ranch there. In 1936, she sold three waterfront acres to newlywed Wolf Bauer, Roche Harbor's chief engineer from 1936 to 1939, for $1,000, a gesture he never forgot. "Ma" Houde once dislodged an apple stuck in a cow's throat and cured a goat of gastritis with a poke in the ribs with a darning needle. (Wolf Bauer collection.)

Clara Tarte was Carrie in the 1966 United Artists film *Namu, the Killer Whale*. The film starred Robert Lansing as marine biologist Hank Donner, who protects Namu after another orca was shot and killed by fishermen. Lee Meriwether costarred as fishing supply store owner Kate Rand. Much of *Namu* was filmed on San Juan Island. Here Clara Tarte gets a kiss from Joe Higgins during a break in filming. (Neil Tarte collection.)

Several island children were cast in *Namu*, among them Steve Buck, getting a hug from Clara Tarte. Buck now owns Coldwell Banker San Juan Island. Clara Tarte was "discovered" by directors while she was tending to her garden. Her grandson, Neil Tarte Jr., also had a part in the film. (Lee Meriwether photograph/Kelley Balcomb-Bartok collection.)

Actor John Wayne visits with Clara Tarte and her daughter, Teresa, at Roche Harbor. Wayne was a frequent visitor to Roche Harbor in his converted minesweeper, the *Wild Goose*, and became a friend of the Tarte family, who developed the resort beginning in 1956. Clara and the actor became close friends. (Teresa Tarte Kennedy collection.)

John Wayne enjoys dinner at Roche Harbor during the Tarte era. It's probably no coincidence that a food dish holder is shaped like a wild goose, in recognition of Wayne and his yacht, the *Wild Goose*, a converted World War II minesweeper. Wayne enjoyed Roche Harbor because, despite his prominence, he was treated as a member of the boating community. (Teresa Tarte Kennedy collection.)

Einar Nielsen (1932–1984) built roads for Roche Harbor Resort, became the resort's vice president, served as a San Juan County commissioner from 1978 to 1979, and was an advocate of restoring a nearby portion of the military road built by the British during the joint military occupation. An annual fishing derby named in his memory raises thousands of dollars for college scholarships for local high school graduates. (Susan Nielsen collection.)

John McMillin built Afterglow Mausoleum for his family. It is rich in Masonic symbolism. The limestone table represents the eternal table at which the family will gather; the chairs are crypts. They are surrounded by seven columns, one of which is missing to represent our unfinished work in life. Steps to the crypts represent stages of life, orders in architecture, the human senses, and the liberal arts and sciences. (Mary McMillin Cooper collection.)

Afterglow Mausoleum has six crypts, but there have been seven inurnments. The ashes of Adah Beeny (1868–1955), the McMillin children's caretaker, were interred in the crypt of the McMillins' infant son, John Hiett McMillin. The last inurnment here was in 1980, after the McMillins' daughter and last surviving child, Dorothy Hiett McMillin, died. The ashes of Adda McMillin, the wife of Paul, were spread at sea off Roche Harbor. (Mary McMillin Cooper collection.)

Afterglow Mausoleum is a significant place. Like any cemetery, it is a sacred and protected place. It is a Masonic landmark and, because of the important Masonic elements in the mausoleum's architecture, the Masonic lodge holds ceremonies here. As the final resting place of Sigma Chi fraternity's first grand consul, the mausoleum's care is monitored by Sigma Chi's Monuments and Memorials Commission.

Seven

THE BIRTH OF THE BOATEL

By 1956, Paul McMillin had worked 50 of his 70 years at Roche Harbor. He led the company through the Depression, labor unrest, and changing markets. Now he was seeing what geologists told him in 1938 to be true: Roche Harbor's limestone would be exhausted. His yacht and the sea beckoning him, he was ready to retire.

Reuben J. Tarte (1901–1968) was born with a touch of Roche Harbor in his blood.

His uncle, Capt. James W. Tarte (1849–1932), operated the *Evangel* and the *Brick* between Seattle, Victoria, and Port Angeles in the 1880s and was likely the skipper when the *Evangel* delivered Philip Clayton Van Buskirk to the Scurr brothers' dock in 1883, in the sailor and diarist's well-documented first attempt to homestead an island in the area.

Like his uncle, Reuben Tarte loved the sea. He and his wife, the former Clara Diaz (1899–1990), became active boaters in 1936, sailing Northwest inland waters in their cruiser, the *Clareu*. When his boat was called into service by the U.S. Navy to patrol Puget Sound during World War II, Tarte was commissioned a lieutenant commander so he could stay behind her helm.

Tarte was also entrepreneurial. He founded Transport Storage and Distributing in Seattle in 1931, and in 1953, he invented the piggyback flatcar to improve the delivery of automobiles by rail. He made a fortune.

Tarte and friends bought a cabin and dock on Garrison Bay for a place to gather before boating north. In nearby Roche Harbor, Tarte saw endless possibilities for a boating resort. Roche Harbor Boatel and Resort was born.

"There was nothing besides fuel docks north of Seattle and no place for boaters to tie up and go ashore," according to *Roche Harbor Resort: A Family Affair*, an unpublished story of the Tartes' ownership produced in the 1990s. "When they heard that Roche Harbor was for sale, they jumped at the chance."

On September 20, 1956, Tarte and his son, Neil, purchased Paul and Adda McMillin's stock in Roche Harbor for about $300,000—almost $2.3 million in 2008 dollars.

Tarte's foresight proved correct: because of his vision and the family's hard work, Roche Harbor is a premier Northwest boating destination, and the family continues to be a part of village life.

According to *Roche Harbor Resort: A Family Affair*, "The Tarte family created more than just a resort, they created a home away from home for their guests where the smiles and laughter were genuine and the friendships made long-lasting."

Sam Buck Sr. of San Juan Properties commissioned this hand-drawn map of the islands, extolling the natural and recreational amenities of the San Juans and Roche Harbor. "The unhurried

atmosphere that abounds in this God-selected site, becomes a way of life to the one who lingers," the map boasted. (Sam Buck Sr. collection.)

The Tarte family moved to Roche Harbor in 1957 to help with construction and gathered for their first Easter portrait at Roche Harbor in 1958. "With an enormous amount of work and family unity, the Tartes were successful in their goal of establishing a resort and, in the summer of 1957, Roche Harbor Resort was opened to the public," according to *Roche Harbor Resort: A Family Affair.* (Teresa Tarte Kennedy collection.)

Reuben and Clara Tarte enjoy an outing on their 50-foot cruiser, the *Clareu.* As reported in *Roche Harbor Resort: A Family Affair,* "With the Tarte family being so active in the boating community, the news of the opening traveled fast. . . . The family was overwhelmed with the amount of business they received the first summer." (Teresa Tarte Kennedy collection.)

Reuben Tarte resurrected the Roche Harbor Yacht Club in 1957. The club was founded by John S. McMillin in 1906 but had been dormant since the beginning of World War II. Twenty-five people joined the club at its first annual meeting on February 22, 1957; today the club has about 200 members. He also donated land for a county park on Limestone Point. The park is named in his honor.

The remains of the tug *Roche Harbor* loom over Neil Tarte, wearing sunglasses and visiting with friends on the beach at the old boatyard around 1960. At right is a scow with the designation *Roche Harbor F.* The 50.4-foot tug was built in 1888 in Tacoma by Harry and Lynn Maloney, who named her the *Harry Lynn.* Only her boiler and propeller remain on the site today.

Tarte family members enjoy an outing at Afterglow Beach around 1958. From left to right are (first row) Betty Clark, Neil Tarte, Byron Halvorson, Margaret Tarte, and Bob Tangney; (second row) unidentified, Teresa Tangney, and Mary Lou Halvorson. "Reuben didn't buy Roche Harbor to make it into a resort," said Sam Buck Sr., a family friend. "He built it to be a haven for boaters. And he wanted a place for his whole family." (Teresa Tarte Kennedy collection.)

The Tartes built the main dock using pilings from cedar cut on Roche Harbor land at Limestone Point. By July 1, 1957, the main dock—with 300 feet of floats and four 90-foot finger floats, enough space for 200 boats—had been completed. An aquatic land lease was acquired for 50 mooring buoys, an idea borrowed from Catalina Island and a first in Washington State. (Teresa Tarte Kennedy collection.)

Roche Harbor gardener F. R. Scott, also known as Scotty, continued with the company during its transition from lime company town to boating resort. On June 5, 1960, the *Seattle Times* wrote, "The gardens surrounding the hotel are in the care of F.R. Scott (shown here tending one of the flower beds). His flowers have won for the hotel 30 San Juan County Fair prizes." (Gwen Bergh Cole collection.)

Margaret and Neil Tarte and their children, Neil Jr., Georgi, Janine, and Sally, pose for a picture in the Hotel de Haro garden around 1962. This picture was taken the day of Sally's first communion. The garden is a popular venue for events, particularly weddings, today. (Neil Tarte collection.)

The Hotel de Haro had been closed since about 1942 and was in need of repair when the Tarte family bought Roche Harbor in 1956. Each family member "was determined to make the best of things . . . and do the hard physical labor necessary to restore the family home and the once grand hotel," wrote Gwen Burgh Cole, who worked summers at the resort while in college. (Teresa Tarte Kennedy collection.)

The Tartes restored the Hotel de Haro and reopened it in 1959 to resort visitors. The hotel, which celebrated its 120th birthday in 2006, is a bridge between Roche Harbor's past, present, and future. The hotel and gardens are still the centerpiece of the village. (Teresa Tarte Kennedy collection.)

The lobby of the Hotel de Haro is pictured shortly after it reopened in 1959. According to the oldest pictures of the hotel, this area was originally a dining room for lime company employees and guests. Visitors can enjoy refreshments near the fireplace and peruse artifacts and photographs from Roche Harbor's colorful history. (Gwen Bergh Cole collection.)

Shortly after the Tartes bought Roche Harbor, Clara Tarte began renovating the church into a Catholic chapel. She obtained pews from a church in West Seattle; candleholders, chalices, and vestments from priest friends; and commissioned a Spanish carver to replicate a statue of Mary she saw on a trip there. She named the church Our Lady of Good Voyage after a church she visited in Massachusetts.

Neil and Margaret Tarte prepare for Mass at Our Lady of Good Voyage around 1995 with children in their family. From left to right are John Schuman, Tim Aylward, Katie Carlton, Heidi Schuman, Sissy Carlton, and Jennifer Wells. (Neil Tarte collection.)

Our Lady of Good Voyage was consecrated by Archbishop Thomas Connelly and is the only privately owned Catholic chapel in the United States. A stained-glass window above the doors was installed in memory of the Tartes' son, Dr. Lawrence Tarte. Carrillon bells were installed and chime three times daily in memory of Reuben Tarte, who died in 1968, and son-in-law Bob Tangney, who died in 1971. (Teresa Tarte Kennedy collection.)

Reuben and Clara Tarte built their home on the former site of the lime company's barrel factory. The expansive waterfront home was the scene of many lively family gatherings. Nancy Tarte Rodriguez-Atkatz dances with her father, Neil, at her wedding reception at the family home on June 1, 1985. (Neil Tarte collection.)

A horse-drawn carriage passes under the sign at the entrance to the resort. The horse stables were located near the former site of the lime company's barrel factory. Neil Tarte said he got the idea for the sign from Furnace Creek Inn and Ranch Resort in Death Valley, California. (Teresa Tarte Kennedy collection.)

Roche Harbor, Washington ● Telephone 378-2313

ENJOY BOATING, SWIMMING, RIDING, FISHING, HUNTING, AND DINING OUT IN THE FINEST SPOT IN THE PACIFIC NORTHWEST FOR AN OUTDOOR VACATION

Complete Recreational Facilities

restaurant . . . boating facilities . . . swimming (fresh and salt water) . . . 4000 ft. runway airport . . . salt water beach . . . yacht club . . . clam digging, crabbing and fishing . . . best harbor available between Shilshole and Alaska.

An early brochure told of all the amenities awaiting guests to Roche Harbor Resort: boating, clamming, crabbing, dining, fishing, hunting, riding, and swimming. Boaters who tied up at mooring buoys were picked up by skiff and delivered to the dock so that they felt no different than a boater with the biggest slip. "The Tartes pampered their guests by offering them every convenience," according to *Roche Harbor Resort: A Family Affair*. (Sam Buck Sr. collection.)

A fleet of planes from a Portland, Oregon, flying club landed at Roche Harbor's airstrip on June 7, 1981. The airstrip was developed in 1960 and immediately proved a tremendous asset to the resort. As *Roche Harbor Resort: A Family Affair* states, "Boaters from out of town . . . could leave their boat moored on the dock and fly out of the harbor on business. Regular passenger service also increased."

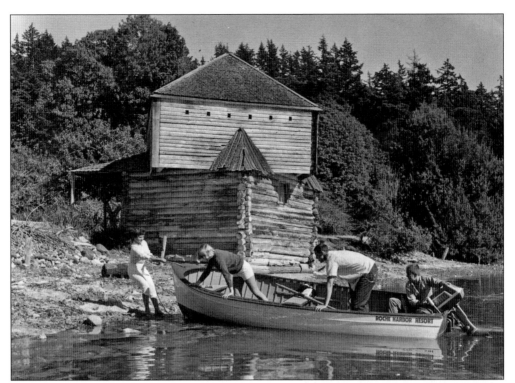

"A favorite boating and beachcombing area for Roche Harbor guests and off-duty employees is Garrison Bay, a short trip south of the harbor," the *Seattle Times* reported in a June 5, 1960, feature. "Stopping at Garrison Bay's most famous landmark, an ancient British blockhouse, were four young Roche Harbor employees, Gwen Bergh, Betsy Neighbor, Bill Brilliant and Kelvin Vogel." (Gwen Bergh Cole collection.)

The Tartes added an ice cream station, at left, after they reopened the Roche Harbor general store. Like today, the store offered groceries, hardware, and marine-related items. (Neil Tarte collection.)

The swimming pool was installed in 1959 on the former site of the lime company's employee cottages; all but nine of the cottages were sold and moved to new sites on the island. The pool was the first built on San Juan Island. Reuben and Clara Tarte's grandchildren pose on the diving board: from left to right are Georgi Tarte, Nancy Tarte, Janine Tarte, Karin Halvorson, Chris Halvorson, Susie Tangney, and Neil Tarte Jr. (Janine Tarte Wells collection.)

Lori Buck walks past the Hotel de Haro in this early 1970s photograph. Her experiences working at Roche Harbor included an outing on John Wayne's boat. Later, Buck told the actor, "Thank you, Mr. Wayne," and he said, "No, thank you, Miss Buck," and kissed her hand. "She said she wouldn't wash that hand for a couple of weeks," her father, Sam Buck Sr., recalled. (Sam Buck Sr. collection.)

Reuben Tarte started Roche Harbor's colors ceremony after watching a similar ceremony at the parliament building in Victoria, British Columbia. The first colors ceremony was reportedly carried out in the opening of the summer season of 1957 by Chuck Jamison, a security officer who had been foreman of the lime plant, and Vic Reynolds, who was the resort's first moorage boy.

As in the beginning, the colors ceremony is carried out by employees, including Tarte family members, from Memorial Day to Labor Day. The ceremony is non-military but recognizes the island's historic ties. Employees proceed to the flagpole to "Colonel Bogey March." The Canadian flag is lowered to "O, Canada." The British flag is lowered to "God Save the Queen." The U.S. flag is lowered to "Taps." (Neil Tarte collection.)

John Wayne clowns in a photograph with Clara Tarte, in striped shirt, and other Tarte family members during a sailing excursion outside Friday Harbor. The actor loved the camaraderie of Roche Harbor. Teresa Tarte Kennedy recalled an outing on Wayne's boat. "We were standing on the fantail and, as Duke looked back at Roche Harbor, he said, 'Teresa, do you realize what your father and mother have done?'" (Teresa Tarte Kennedy collection.)

Roche Harbor's gazebo lounge is built on the former site of John and Louella McMillin's open gazebo. It was built in 1975 to accommodate live entertainment as well as dining. "Neil patterned the lounge after the gazebo that John S. had and worked extremely hard to match the wood pattern exactly so that it looked original and like it belonged," according to *Roche Harbor Resort: A Family Affair.*

From left to right, the USS *Implicit* AM-455, USS *Esteem* AM-438, and the USS *Conquest* AM-488 visited Roche Harbor on July 4, 1976, for the nation's bicentennial. The minesweepers were invited by Neil Tarte, then-president of Roche Harbor Resort. The visit was a reminder of Reuben Tarte's service patrolling Puget Sound in his *Clareu* during World War II. (Neil Tarte collection.)

Thousands of visitors are drawn to Roche Harbor's annual Fourth of July festivities. The day's activities include a blindfolded dinghy race, donut-eating contest, fun run, logrolling contest, election of the honorary mayor, and the fireworks show. (Neil Tarte collection.)

In 1997, the addition of more docks and slips enabled Roche Harbor to accommodate 377 vessels. "Great care was taken to make sure the new docks would portray the same ambiance of the historical buildings around the harbor with the addition of Victorian lamps lining the wide wooden main pier," Roche Harbor's Web site states. (Neil Tarte collection.)

Roche Harbor's Fourth of July fireworks show is an annual tradition that leaves indelible memories. Today several of Reuben and Clara Tarte's grandchildren and great-grandchildren work at Roche Harbor, contributing to the feel of continuity in a changing community. Teresa Tarte Kennedy said of Roche Harbor and her family, "This is where it begins and ends." (Neil Tarte collection.)

Eight

THE VILLAGE ERA

In 1988, the Tarte family sold Roche Harbor Resort to Verne Howard, the owner of grocery stores in Friday Harbor and Idaho; and Rich Komen, the founder of Restaurants Unlimited. Howard and Komen also purchased the Cowells' minority shares, held by the Cowell Foundation, ending the Cowells' 100-year association with Roche Harbor. In 1997, Howard sold his shares to Saltchuk Resources, which owns air cargo, marine transportation, petroleum distribution, and real estate companies.

In the first decade of the 21st century, Roche Harbor began implementing Komen's vision of a year-round village in addition to a seasonal destination.

In 2005, a neighborhood of early 1900s-style homes was completed along McMillin Drive, which leads from Roche Harbor Road to the Hotel de Haro.

In 2007, the traditional neighborhood grew to include five 1900s-style, harbor-view townhomes. Also in 2007, construction began on 17 homes, termed "woodland cottages," off Roche Harbor Road. Design guidelines regulate such building details as paint color, type of windows and roof pitch, so the neighborhood blends in with Roche Harbor's historic architectural elements.

On July 2, 2007, Quarryman Hall opened adjacent to the Hotel de Haro. Quarryman Hall was a $4.5-million project. It has 12 guest suites, retail shops, and a spa. Hotel de Haro is the subject of continued restoration.

Today the village is a well-rounded community offering a variety of life-enriching activities. A growing population of year-round residents enjoys such amenities as a post office, retail shops, a spa, and three restaurants, two of which are in John and Louella McMillin's former home.

The marina has an international feel, with U.S. Customs stationed here and boats of all sizes arriving from or going to Canada. The marina is also home to several people who live on their boats. Kayakers depart from here to Yellow Island to see wildflowers or the west side to see orcas and other marine life. Anglers compete in two major sport-fishing events, the Einar Nielsen/Becky Barr Fishing Derby in September and the Roche Harbor Salmon Classic Invitational in February.

Hiking trails lead to heritage sites and through the now-lush former quarries. Roche Harbor Amphitheater and the Roche Harbor Pavilion host live entertainment. Westcott Bay Sculpture Park is a 19-acre site overlooking forests, meadows, rocky outcroppings, and wetlands; trails are interspersed with a rotating exhibit of more than 100 sculptures.

Despite this era of seeming newness, history has actually come full circle: Roche Harbor—originally the village of Whelaalk, then a lime company town, then a boating resort—is again a year-round village of people.

Newlyweds walk down the yellow brick road between the Hotel de Haro gardens; at the time of this writing, Roche Harbor Village accommodates an average of 50 weddings a year. Neil Tarte built the yellow brick road beginning in 1971. He used firebricks that had lined the kilns; many of the bricks bear the names of their manufacturers. (Marie DiCristina collection.)

Kayaks pass in front of the McMillin Dining Room and Gazebo Lounge en route to a sea adventure. Roche Harbor is a good place to depart for those kayaking to Lime Kiln State Park on the island's west side, where orcas are commonly seen. Yellow Island is another popular kayaking destination; the 11-acre island is home to more than 50 species of wildflowers.

This is the view of the garden and store that John and Louella McMillin enjoyed from their home. But instead of the hustle and bustle of industry, the street in front of the store now teems with artists, live entertainment, and refreshments during the summer months. (Marie DiCristina collection.)

Past, present, and future meld in this street scene: the Hotel de Haro, built in 1886 during the lime era, and Quarryman Hall, built in 2007 during the village era. The hotel offers 20 guest rooms, and Quarryman Hall offers 12 suites. Guests can also stay in one of 21 resort-era condos, 14 village-era homes, nine McMillin-era cottages, and four suites in Paul McMillin's former home. (Marie DiCristina collection.)

Visitors to the Hotel de Haro enjoy this view of the yellow brick road, the gardens, the store, the post office, and the Lime Kiln Cafe, which was originally part of the Tacoma and Roche Harbor Lime Company warehouse. This scene would have been familiar to guests in the early 1900s. (Marie DiCristina collection.)

Quarryman Hall opened in 2007 next to the Hotel de Haro. The designers incorporated early-1900s architectural elements into the building's design so that it blends in with its historic environment. (Author's collection.)

Two visitors enjoy an afternoon stroll on the dock. Roche Harbor's marina is picturesque with a sense of excitement. This is a port of entry, and boats traveling to and from Canada clear customs here. There are 377 slips and a gas dock. Residents and visitors can buy crab and shrimp from local fishermen.

Coast Salish canoes returned to Roche Harbor's shores during the Canoe Journey in 2004. This Swinomish canoe is backdropped by the Hotel de Haro, wharf, and marina. Lummi, Samish, and Swinomish canoe families visited here en route to the territory of the Chemainus First Nation on Vancouver Island in 2004. Languages were spoken and songs were offered here on ancestral ground. (Author's collection.)

A resident walks her bike in a neighborhood of 1900s-style homes on McMillin Drive, which leads into the village, and the Hotel de Haro. These 1900s-style homes were completed in 2005; in 2007, the neighborhood grew to include five harbor-view townhomes, and construction began on 17 woodland cottages on Roche Harbor Road.

Residents and guests enjoy views like this from the townhomes between the village homes and the Hotel de Haro. Visible here are the marina, store, wharf, and, in the distance, Henry Island. Steps leading to a lush neighborhood park date to 1898 and were the steps that led to Dr. Victor J. Capron's home, which no longer exists.

Westcott Bay Sculpture Park opened in 2001 on what was once a baseball field and, before that, part of John S. McMillin's Bellevue Farm. The 19-acre site overlooks forests, meadows, rocky outcroppings, and wetlands. The outdoor museum features a rotating exhibit of more than 100 sculptures, among them works in bronze, ceramic, glass, metal, stone, and wood by noted artists from around the world. (Nina Pellar LeBaron collection.)

Kate Wisniewski was Dromio and Daniel Mayes was Antipholus in Island Stage Left's Wild West version of Shakespeare's A Comedy of Errors from July 12 to August 5, 2007, in Roche Harbor's amphitheater. The amphitheater, which opened in July 2006 with Island Stage Left's Merchant of Venice, is a significant cultural offering for local residents as well as islanders. Island Stage Left often performs in the Roche Harbor Pavilion as well. (John Sinclair collection.)

BIBLIOGRAPHY

Dailey, Tom, et al. *Coast Salish Villages of Puget Sound.* coastsalishmap.org

Keddie, Grant. *Songhees Pictorial: A History of the Songhees People as Seen by Outsiders, 1790–1912.* Victoria, B.C.: Royal British Columbia Museum, 2003.

Lopez Island Historical Society. *Everett Morning Tribune,* "Islands of San Juan County, Washington," July 18, 1908, special section. Reprinted 1976.

McCormick, John A. *Cruise of the Calcite.* Everett, WA: B&E Enterprises, 1973.

Richardson, David B. *Pig War Islands.* Eastsound, WA: Orcas Publishing Company, 1971.

The Royal Engineers Living History Group. *The Royal Engineers in Her Britannic Majesty's Colonies of Vancouver's Island and British Columbia.* www.royalengineers.ca

Stein, Julie K. *Exploring Coast Salish Prehistory: The Archaeology of San Juan Island.* Seattle: University of Washington Press, 2000.

Suttles, Wayne Prescott. *Economic Life of the Coast Salish of Haro and Rosario Straits.* Seattle: University of Washington Press, 1951.

Vouri, Michael. *Outpost of Empire: The Royal Marines and the Joint Occupation of San Juan Island.* Seattle: Northwest Interpretive Association/University of Washington, 2004.

The *West Shore* magazine, "One Thousand Barrels a Day," August 1889.

Wilhelm, Honor. *Illustrated Supplement to the San Juan Islander, 1901.* Seattle: Shorey Book Store, 1966.

Wright, E. W., ed. *Lewis and Dryden's Marine History of the Pacific Northwest.* Portland, OR: Lewis and Dryden Printing Company, 1895.

ACROSS AMERICA, PEOPLE ARE DISCOVERING
SOMETHING WONDERFUL. *THEIR HERITAGE.*

Arcadia Publishing is the leading local history publisher in the United States. With more than 5,000 titles in print and hundreds of new titles released every year, Arcadia has extensive specialized experience chronicling the history of communities and celebrating America's hidden stories, bringing to life the people, places, and events from the past. To discover the history of other communities across the nation, please visit:

www.arcadiapublishing.com

Customized search tools allow you to find regional history books about the town where you grew up, the cities where your friends and family live, the town where your parents met, or even that retirement spot you've been dreaming about.

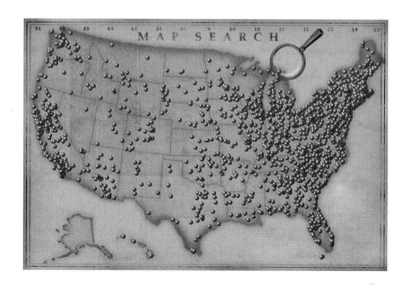